NOVEL EXPERIENCES

NOVEL EXPERIENCES
Literature Units for Book Discussion Groups
in the Elementary Grades

CHRISTINE JENKINS and SALLY FREEMAN

Illustrated by
Lawrence Freeman

1991
TEACHER IDEAS PRESS
A Division of
Libraries Unlimited, Inc.
Englewood, Colorado

KINGSVILLE PUBLIC LIBRARY
P.O. BOX 57
KINGSVILLE, OH 44048

Copyright © 1991 Libraries Unlimited, Inc.
All Rights Reserved
Printed in the United States of America

No part of this publication may be reproduced, stored in a retrieval system, or transmitted, in any form or by any means, electronic, mechanical, photocopying, recording, or otherwise, without the prior written permission of the publisher. An exception is made for individual library media specialists and teachers who may make copies of activity sheets for classroom use in a single school. Other portions of the book (up to 15 pages) may be copied for in-service programs or other educational programs in a single school.

TEACHER IDEAS PRESS
A Division of
Libraries Unlimited, Inc.
P.O. Box 3988
Englewood, Colorado 80155-3988

Suggested Cataloging:

Jenkins, Christine, 1949-
　　Novel experiences : literature units for book discussion groups in the elementary grades / Christine Jenkins and Sally Freeman ; illustrated by Lawrence Freeman. — Englewood, Colo.: Teacher Ideas Press, 1991.
　　v, 231 p. 22x28 cm.
　　ISBN 0-87287-730-2
　　1. Reading (Elementary)--United States--Language experience approach. 2. Language arts (Elementary)--United States. 3. Children--United States--Books and reading. I. Freeman, Sally. II. Freeman, Lawrence. III. Title.
LB1050.36.J2　　1991
028.5'35

Contents

Introduction ... 1

GRADE TWO
The Beast in Ms. Rooney's Room ... 5
The Gingerbread Rabbit ... 10
Julian's Glorious Summer ... 17
Jumanji ... 22
Nate the Great and the Fishy Prize ... 25
Something Queer at the Library ... 29
Wagon Wheels ... 33

GRADE THREE
Altogether, One at a Time ... 39
The Celery Stalks at Midnight ... 44
The Hundred Dresses ... 50
On the Banks of Plum Creek ... 55
Sidewalk Story ... 65
Stone Fox ... 68
A Taste of Blackberries ... 72

GRADE FOUR
Follow My Leader ... 77
Homer Price ... 83
Jennifer, Hecate, Macbeth, William McKinley, and Me, Elizabeth ... 91
Knight's Castle ... 97
Mrs. Piggle-Wiggle's Magic ... 105
Sadako and the Thousand Paper Cranes ... 113
Song of the Trees ... 118

GRADE FIVE
The Egypt Game ... 123
Gone-Away Lake ... 130
Harriet Tubman: Conductor on the Underground Railroad ... 136
In the Year of the Boar and Jackie Robinson ... 146
The Indian in the Cupboard ... 153
Mail-Order Wings ... 162
On My Honor ... 168

GRADE SIX
Dragonwings ... 173
The Hero and the Crown ... 182
Homecoming ... 192
Homesick: My Own Story ... 199
Nobody's Family Is Going to Change ... 207
Roll of Thunder, Hear My Cry ... 216
Sing Down the Moon ... 223

Author/Title Index ... 231

Introduction

As the elementary language arts curriculum moves away from a strict basal reader approach, classroom book discussion groups are becoming increasingly important. Children's literature is a fundamental part of the contemporary elementary language arts curriculum. Its inclusion can and should benefit students in a number of ways. Literature is used in a reading program to expand student experience, help students gain the necessary skills to talk about literature, give them ways to continue their enjoyment of a book, encourage independent reading, and provide a base for future reading experiences. Above all, reading a work of literature and exploring one's thoughts and reactions with others should be an enjoyable and rewarding experience.

In book discussion groups, students do not merely answer recall questions—they work together to discern the meaning of the text and, in doing so, develop higher-level comprehension skills. Many children enjoy talking about what they have read but have a hard time getting beyond "I liked the part where . . ." and "I didn't like the part where . . ." Good book discussions do not just happen. Neither are they only the product of brilliant discussion leaders and gifted students. Good book discussions develop from good discussion questions.

Good discussion questions are specific to the story. For example, instead of asking, "What kind of character is Goldilocks?" the leader might ask group members, "Why do you think Goldilocks always chose the biggest chair and bowl and bed first?" The leader then asks students to support their answers with examples from the text. Good discussion questions are more than factual recall questions and should encourage a *variety* of responses based upon each group member's interpretation of the story. The leader is there to facilitate the discussion by keeping it focused on the text at hand. In most cases this means focusing on the experience of the story rather than on the child's personal experiences. Instead of asking, "Have you ever done the kinds of things that Goldilocks did?" the leader might say, "Why do you think it is always the baby bear's things that Goldilocks disturbs?" Good discussion questions help children focus their thoughts and reactions to the text.*

Book discussion groups organized around student interest rather than reading ability provide a respite from skill-based instructional grouping. We believe that reading groups based on a common interest in a particular book are more successful than groups based solely on student reading level. We have observed that students' interest in reading and discussing what they read is greater when they are offered a choice of books. It is not necessary that all students read the entire book entirely on their own to have a successful book discussion group. The group leader may read the selection aloud, pairs of students may read together, or students may listen to recorded tapes of the selection.

A good book discussion guide must meet several criteria to be truly effective. It should not be too short and superficial, and yet it should not be so long and detailed that it "beats the book to death" and turns a book discussion into another basal reading group. The pre-reading activities should motivate and provide information needed to understand the story. The questions and activities should be geared toward higher-level thinking skills, beyond simple fact retention, and should seek to expand the experience of the book. This expansion, however, should relate directly to the book. (*Charlotte's Web* might lead a student to some further reading on state fairs, but researching the location and dates of state fairs around the country seems like unrelated

---

*If you are looking for information on becoming an effective book discussion leader, we highly recommend Junior Great Books leadership training. The Great Books Foundation sponsors classes throughout the U.S. The Foundation's address is 40 E. Huron, Chicago, IL 60611, and the telephone number is 1-800-222-5870.

busy work to most students.) Many literature guides currently on the market seek to create an entire language arts program from the experience of the novel. Certainly students need to learn phonics, structural analysis, and other reading skills, but requiring them to circle all of the compound words in chapter 6 of *Charlotte's Web* would be an inappropriate use of children's literature.

Novel Experiences contains leader guides for thirty-five books, seven for each grade two through six. In assigning grade levels to these books, we took into consideration the interests and developmental stages of children in the various grades, but discussion leaders should not be limited by our grade designations when choosing a book for a particular group or child. Each book is both worthy of discussion and of high literary quality. The seven books at each grade level include a variety of genres, writing styles, and reading levels. In making our selections, we maintained a balance of male and female main characters. In addition, even with the limited number of titles available in paperback editions, we still tried to choose books representing a wide variety of student backgrounds as we feel it is important to keep a multicultural perspective when choosing books for discussion. Books and reading should be an inclusive experience for *all* students, and children should be encouraged to read about a variety of people and situations to better appreciate the multicultural heritage reflected in our schools.

Each book unit contains the following elements:

Summary. We have written a brief summary for the leader who is unfamiliar with the book. Each summary includes just enough of the plot, characters, and other information to help determine if the book will suit the leader's purposes.

Pre-reading/Motivational Activities. These are activities to be used by the discussion leader to provide students with background information (historical background, geographic location, genre information, etc.) needed to read and understand the story. Selection of activities should depend on the knowledge and experiences of the students in the group. It is not our intention that all activities should be done for each book. In presenting pre-reading activities, it is better to err on the side of brevity.

Vocabulary/Discussion Questions. We have divided the longer books into sections that reflect logical breaks in the book's plot and action and are of a manageable length for student reading and comprehension.

Vocabulary. There is a fairly inclusive list of vocabulary words/phrases for each selection. Our intent is to give the leader information students may need to understand the text and to give an idea of the difficulty and the literary qualities of the work. Some books have specialized vocabularies (legal terms, equestrian terms). Others have vocabulary particular to that book alone (invented language). It is not our intent students be required to labor over the vocabulary before reading the text. The meanings of most of these words will be evident from the context in which they appear. Students should be encouraged to learn the meaning of words that impede comprehension but should *not* be forced to look up long lists of words, use them in sentences, use them for spelling lists, etc. Again, these novels are not workbooks and should not be used as such. Students should enjoy the reading experience.

Discussion Questions. The questions serve as a springboard for group discussion. The leader should not feel compelled to ask all of the questions, but to use those of genuine interest to the leader. There are no right or wrong answers to these questions as long as the students can support their responses with evidence from the text. The questions are specific to the story to help students focus on the book. The discussion should include literary elements, such as plot, characterization, setting, point of view, author's purpose, tone, theme, language, and characteristics of the genre. Remember, sometimes student-generated questions are the best of all.

Enrichment Activities. We provide a variety of multisensory activities to capitalize on the strengths and interests of individual students. Students will be more interested and motivated in their projects if allowed to choose their own activities. The purpose of an enrichment activity is to expand the experience of the book. Good activities relate directly to the text and reflect the meaning of the book to its readers. Such activities enable the students to continue their enjoyment of the book. We have placed the enrichment activities on a separate sheet of paper so they can be duplicated and given to students.

Related Books. The bibliography for each unit includes books and other materials to support the pre-reading and enrichment activities. We have also included an extensive list of other books by the author.

GRADE TWO

The Beast in Ms. Rooney's Room

Author: Patricia Reilley Giff

Illustrator: Blanche Sims

Publisher, Date: Dell, 1984

Pages: 76

SUMMARY

To his dismay, Richard "Beast" Best has been held back in third grade. The adjustment is difficult, but in the first month of school he makes several new friends, learns to read better, and helps his class win the school banner. This realistic novel is the first in the author's 12-book Kids of the Polk Street School series.

PRE-READING/MOTIVATIONAL ACTIVITIES

1. Ask the students to read the title and look at the picture on the cover of the book. Ask them these questions:
   What do you think the Beast in the title is?
   What do you think the story is going to be about?
   Where do you think this story takes place?

2. Ask the group members to think about what their first day of school was like. What did they see? Smell? Hear? Touch? Taste? How did they feel? (Ask the students to write short paragraphs about this and then share them with the other members of the group.)

VOCABULARY/DISCUSSION QUESTIONS

Chapters 1-5:

Vocabulary:

left-back (p. 2)
beast (p. 4)
monitor (p. 7)
midget (p. 8)

call the roll (p. 2)
banner (p. 6)
cafeteria (p. 7)
shin (p. 11)

(vocabulary continues on next page)

6 / The Beast in Ms. Rooney's Room

sauerkraut (p. 19)
assembly (p. 23)
swiveled (p. 28)
Olympics (p. 34)

asparagus (p. 19)
auditorium (p. 24)
somersaults (p. 34)
dried figs (p. 34)

Questions:

1. Why do you think Richard was kept back in third grade?

2. Why did Richard stick an eraser up his nose after he sat down in his seat the first day of school?

3. Why did Richard say "beast" when Ms. Rooney called his name during roll call?

4. When Richard was talking to his old classmates, why do you think he made up the story about why he was "left-back" in third grade?

5. How is Richard's relationship with Mrs. Paris different than his relationship with Ms. Rooney? Why?

6. How do you think Ms. Rooney feels about having Richard in her class again?

Chapters 6-10:

Vocabulary:

President James K. Polk (p. 41)
aisle (p. 46)
thermometer (p. 58)

remedial (p. 43)
Fluffernutter (p. 53)
looseleaf book (p. 66)

Questions:

1. Why do you think Richard keeps getting into trouble?

2. Why does Richard lie about his reading when he talks to Drake at the library?

3. Why does Richard throw the paper airplanes out of the nurse's office window?

4. Do you think Richard became friends with the children in his class because of changes in himself or because of changes in them?

5. Why is winning the banner so important to Emily and Richard?

6. What effect does winning the banner have on the children in the special reading class?

7. Why is Richard a more successful reader at the end of the story than he was at the beginning of the story?

8. How does the meaning of Richard's nickname, Beast, change throughout the story?

9. Why does Richard feel better about being in third grade at the end of the story?

10. At the beginning of the story Richard feels that Ms. Rooney's class is not his "real" class. At what point does Ms. Rooney's class become his "real" class?

11. Why do you think there is a drawing of a paper airplane at the beginning of each chapter?

12. Look at the book's illustrations. How does the artwork reflect the text? Why do you think the artist chose to illustrate those particular events in the story? Which events would you have chosen to illustrate?

RELATED BOOKS

Other books in the Kids of the Polk Street School series:
    The Candy Corn Contest, 1984.
    December Secrets, 1984.
    Fish Face, 1984.
    In the Dinosaur's Paw, 1985.
    Lazy Lions, Lucky Lambs, 1985.
    Pickle Puss, 1986.
    Purple Climbing Days, 1985.
    Say "Cheese", 1985.
    Snaggle Doodles, 1985.
    Sunny-Side Up, 1986.
    The Valentine Star, 1985.

Giff, Patricia Reilly. *The Mystery of the Blue Ring.* New York: Dell, 1987.
    Other books in the Polka Dot Private Eye series:
        The Riddle of the Red Purse, 1987.
        The Secret at the Polk Street School, 1987.
        The Powder Puff Puzzle, 1987.

_____. *Today Was a Terrible Day.* New York: Viking, 1980.
    Other books in the Ronald Morgan series:
        Almost Awful Play, 1985.
        Happy Birthday, Ronald Morgan, 1988.
        Ronald Morgan Goes to Bat, 1988.
        Watch Out, Ronald Morgan!, 1986.

_____. *Watch Out! Man-eating Snake.* New York: Dell, 1988.
    Other books in the New Kids at the Polk Street School series:
        Fancy Feet, 1988.

Books in the Stepping Stones series:

Bulla, Clyde Robert. *The Chalk Box Kid*. New York: Random House, 1987.

Cameron, Ann. *Julian, Secret Agent*. New York: Random House, 1988.

Etra, Jonathan, and Stephanie Spinner. *Aliens for Breakfast*. New York: Random House, 1988.

Hooks, William H. *Pioneer Cat*. New York: Random House, 1988.

Marzollo, Jean. *Red Ribbon Rosie*. New York: Random House, 1988.

O'Connor, Jim, and Jane O'Connor. *The Ghost in Tent 19*. New York: Random House, 1988.

Saunders, Susan. *The Daring Rescue of Marlon the Swimming Pig*. New York: Random House, 1987.

Shreve, Susan. *Lily and the Runaway Baby*. New York: Random House, 1987.

Skurzynski, Gloria. *The Minstrel in the Tower*. New York: Random House, 1988.

Stevenson, Jocelyn. *O'Diddy*. New York: Random House, 1988.

Whelan, Gloria. *Next Spring an Oriole*. New York: Random House, 1987.

_____. *Silver*. New York: Random House, 1988.

Yep, Laurence. *The Curse of the Squirrel*. New York: Random House, 1987.

ENRICHMENT ACTIVITIES

The Beast in Ms. Rooney's Room

1. Design a school banner.

2. Read other books in the Kids of the Polk Street School series (see Related Books).

3. Make a map of your classroom similar to the one at the beginning of the book.

4. Do you think it's a good idea to retain someone in the third grade? Divide a paper in two. Write the arguments *for* retaining someone on one side and the arguments *against* retaining someone on the other side. What is your conclusion? Write it at the bottom of your paper.

5. Write a name poem describing Richard "Beast" Best, Emily, and Drake.

B	E	D
E	M	R
A	I	A
S	L	K
T	Y	E

6. Write a letter or card that Richard might have sent to Mrs. Paris at the end of the year.

7. The school in the book was named for President James K. Polk. Find out when he was president and what happened while he was president. Write a short report and share the information with the class.

8. Ask 10 other children how old they were when they lost their first tooth. Make a graph or chart of the information.

9. Create your own activity for *The Beast in Ms. Rooney's Room*.

The Gingerbread Rabbit

Author: Randall Jarrell

Illustrator: Garth Williams

Publisher, Date: Collier/Macmillan, 1964

Pages: 55

SUMMARY

A mother sets out to bake a gingerbread rabbit for her daughter, but the rabbit runs away! This humorous story follows the rabbit's adventures as he is pursued by both the mother and a hungry fox and eventually finds a home with a loving pair of real rabbits.

PRE-READING/MOTIVATIONAL ACTIVITIES

1. Read *The Gingerbread Man* together. Do a story map of *The Gingerbread Man* (see Figure 1). Explain to the group that *The Gingerbread Rabbit* is based on the familiar tale, *The Gingerbread Man*, and that you will be discussing their similarities and differences later.

2. Ask the students to read the title and look at the picture on the cover of the book. Ask them these questions:
    What do you think the story is going to be about?
    Who do you think the main characters are going to be?
    What do you think is the setting of the story?

Fig. 1. Sample Story Maps
Title: *The Gingerbread Man*
Author: Karen Schmidt
Setting: Time—One day
         Place—Cottage and the fields around it
Main Character: Gingerbread man
Problem: The gingerbread man has escaped from the oven and many other story characters are trying to catch him.

Goal (of the main character): The gingerbread man wants to get away from all of the other characters in the story.

Episodes:
1. The old woman puts the gingerbread man into the oven.
2. The boy opens the oven and the gingerbread man escapes.
3. The boy, old woman, and old man chase him, but he escapes.
4. The farmers chase him, but he escapes.

5. The bear chases him, but he escapes.
6. The wolf chases him, but he escapes.
7. The fox tricks the gingerbread man into coming close to him.

Resolution: The fox eats the gingerbread man.

Title: *The Gingerbread Rabbit*
Author: Randall Jarrell
Setting: Time—School day in present time
        Place—Cottage and woods around it
Main Characters: Gingerbread rabbit, mother

Problem: Mother makes the gingerbread rabbit for her little girl, but the gingerbread rabbit is afraid he will be eaten and runs away.

Goal (of the main character): Gingerbread rabbit wants to escape from the mother so he won't be eaten.

Episodes:
1. The mother leaves the rabbit on the table while she goes to see the vegetable man.
2. The paring knife, bowl, and rolling pin tell the rabbit he is going to be eaten.
3. The rabbit runs away, with the mother close behind.
4. The squirrel tries to help the rabbit and then tells the mother why the rabbit is running away.
5. The fox tries to trick the rabbit into going into his hole.
6. The real rabbit saves the gingerbread rabbit from the fox.

Resolution: The gingerbread rabbit escapes from the mother and the fox and goes to live with the real rabbits.

VOCABULARY/DISCUSSION QUESTIONS

Vocabulary:

paring knife (p. 2)
molasses (p. 2)
vegetable man (p. 4)
delicate (p. 10)
complacent (p. 10)
cater-cornered (p. 12)
pant (p. 15)
bedclothes (p. 19)
cannibal (p. 26)
exhaust (p. 27)
confirmed (p. 28)
innocent (p. 28)
absurd (p. 31)
cordially (p. 31)
gnaw (p. 32)
watercress (p. 37)
sulkily (p. 45)

trousers (p. 2)
blanched almond (p. 4)
slender (p. 10)
edible (p. 10)
wistfully (p. 11)
tremendous (p. 12)
burrow (p. 19)
bounded (p. 23)
unseasonably (p. 27)
enormity (p. 28)
vegetarian (p. 28)
scoundrel (p. 31)
atrocious (p. 31)
propose (p. 31)
rushes (p. 37)
uncertainly (p. 41)
discontented (p. 45)

12 / The Gingerbread Rabbit

Questions:

1. Why do you think the mother said, "Do you think I'm a cannibal?" (p. 26)

2. Reread page 10. Why do the bowl, rolling pin, and knife think the rabbit is not beautiful?

3. When the objects are talking to the rabbit do you think they are being cruel or honest or both? Explain.

4. Why is this rabbit so important to the mother? Why do you think she doesn't simply make another one?

5. Who helps the rabbit the most? Explain.

6. Both the mother and the fox chase the gingerbread rabbit. How else are they alike?

7. Which character is the most unselfish? Explain.

8. Reread page 55. Why do the rabbits revisit the house? Why don't the two big rabbits explain the "giant" to the gingerbread rabbit? Why do all three of them say, "Good-bye, old giant"?

9. Do a story map of *The Gingerbread Rabbit* (see Figure 1). Compare the story maps for *The Gingerbread Man* and *The Gingerbread Rabbit*.

10. Look at the book's illustrations. How does the artwork reflect the text? Why do you think the artist chose to illustrate those particular events in the story? Which events would you have chosen to illustrate?

RELATED BOOKS

Brown, Margaret Wise. *Little Fur Family*. New York: Harper, 1946.

———. *The Runaway Bunny*. New York: Harper, 1942.

———. *Three Little Animals*. New York: Harper, 1956.

———. *Wait Till the Moon Is Full*. New York: Harper, 1948.

Galdone, Paul (illustrator). *The Gingerbread Boy*. Boston: Houghton Mifflin, 1983.

Jarrell, Randall. *The Animal Family*. New York: Pantheon, 1965.

_____. *The Bat-Poet*. New York: Macmillan, 1964.

_____. *The Fisherman and His Wife: A Tale from the Brothers Grimm*. New York: Farrar, Straus, Giroux, 1980.

_____. *Fly by Night*. New York: Farrar, Straus, Giroux, 1980.

Schmidt, Karen (illustrator). *The Gingerbread Man*. New York: Scholastic, 1985.

ENRICHMENT ACTIVITIES

The Gingerbread Rabbit

1. Reread *The Gingerbread Man* and the story maps of both stories. Divide a piece of paper in half down the middle. Write "Alike" on one side and "Different" on the other side. Under "Alike" write how the two stories are the same, and under "Different" write how the two stories are different. Share your lists with the group.

2. Write another runaway gingerbread story, such as
   The Gingerbread Ant
   The Gingerbread Dinosaur
   The Gingerbread Tractor

3. Make a stuffed gingerbread rabbit out of felt (see pattern on page 16).

4. Make gingerbread rabbits (see recipe below).

5. Rewrite the story as a puppet play. Perform it.

6. Make a diorama of the rabbit burrow.

7. Make a map of the gingerbread rabbit's journey.

8. Read *The Runaway Bunny* by Margaret Wise Brown. Tell the group how the stories are alike and different.

9. Create your own activity for *The Gingerbread Rabbit*.

Gingerbread Rabbits

¾ cup unsulphured molasses

¾ cup butter

¾ cup dark brown sugar

4½ cups flour

1 teaspoon baking powder

1 teaspoon salt

½ teaspoon baking soda

2 teaspoons ground ginger

2 teaspoons cinnamon

1 egg, beaten

1. Heat the molasses until it simmers, remove from heat, and stir in the butter until it melts. Stir in the brown sugar. Cool.

2. Sift together the flour, baking powder, salt, baking soda, ginger, and cinnamon. Stir, along with the egg, into the cooled molasses mixture. Mix well. Wrap in waxed paper and chill 1-2 hours, or until firm enough to roll.

3. Preheat the oven to 350 degrees.

4. Roll out the dough to ¼-inch thickness on a lightly floured board or pastry cloth. Cut with a rabbit-shaped cookie cutter.

5. Transfer to a lightly greased baking sheet and bake 12-15 minutes. Cool on a rack. The gingerbread rabbits may be decorated with icing, candies, and raisins.

16 / The Gingerbread Rabbit

Stuffed Gingerbread Rabbit
Pattern and Directions

Materials: gingerbread rabbit pattern (below)

2 pieces dark brown felt, each measuring about 7 inches by 4 inches

pins

scissors

three tiny buttons for eyes and mouth

fabric glue

needle and thread

polyester fiberfill

1. Cut out the pattern and pin it to a piece of dark brown felt. Cut carefully around the pattern. This is the front of the rabbit. Repeat to make the back of the rabbit.

2. Glue or sew the mouth and eyes onto the front of the rabbit.

3. Place the front and back pieces together. Begin sewing the pieces together almost all the way around the rabbit but leave a 2-inch gap on the side. Be sure to tie a knot in the thread so that your rabbit doesn't lose its stuffing.

4. Stuff the rabbit with polyester fiberfill. Finish sewing the side together. Don't forget to tie the knot!

Love your bunny!

Julian's Glorious Summer

Author: Ann Cameron

Illustrator: Dora Leder

Publisher, Date: Random House, 1987

Pages: 62

SUMMARY

Julian's glorious summer has just begun and already he has problems. His best friend, Gloria, has a new blue bicycle, and he can't bring himself to tell her that he is afraid to learn to ride. One lie leads to another, and it begins to look like Julian's glorious summer will be ruined.

PRE-READING/MOTIVATIONAL ACTIVITIES

1. Ask the students to discuss and/or write about the question: Have you ever wanted to do something new but been afraid to try?

2. Discuss how we all feel on the first day of summer vacation. Be sure to include positive and negative feelings.

3. Ask the students to read the title and look at the picture on the cover of the book. Ask them these questions:
   What do you think the story is going to be about?
   Who do you think the main characters are going to be?
   What do you think is the setting of the story?

VOCABULARY/DISCUSSION QUESTIONS

Chapters 1-2:

Vocabulary:

glorious (title)
concentrating (p. 8)
reverse boomerang wish (p. 10)
enthusiastic (p. 13)
permanent (p. 14)

absolutely (p. 5)
embarrassed (p. 9)
congratulate (p. 12)
streamers (p. 13)
asteroid (p. 18)

18 / Julian's Glorious Summer

Questions:

1. Why do you think Julian tells Gloria he has to work all summer?

2. Does Gloria believe him? Why or why not?

3. Prediction: What do you think is going to happen to Julian this summer?

Chapters 3-6:

Vocabulary:

definitely (p. 28)
eaves (p. 31)
national disaster (p. 41)

opportunity (p. 30)
electric-eye doors (p. 37)

Questions:

1. Why do you think Julian won't just admit that he is afraid?

2. Why is Julian's father angry about Julian's telling Gloria he had to work all summer?

3. "My words came out all white and thin, like a little skinny piece of spaghetti." (p. 25) What does this mean?

4. Why does Julian's father call the work Julian is doing an "opportunity"? (p. 30)

5. Julian's father gave him a great deal of work to do. Do you think he is being fair? Why or why not?

6. Julian's mother tells him, "Suffering is the beginning of happiness." (p. 40) What does she mean?

Chapters 7-9:

Vocabulary:

tiptoppiest (p. 48)
foundation (p. 49)
Grand Canyon (p. 58)

Mount Everest (p. 48)
scooter (p. 57)

Questions:

1. Why does Julian decide to keep the bicycle?

2. If father had told mother that he was going to buy Julian a bike, what do you think she would have said to him?

3. Why does Julian finally admit to Gloria that he is afraid to ride the bicycle?

4. What makes Julian change his mind about riding the bicycle?

5. Look at the book's illustrations. How does the artwork reflect the text? Why do you think the artist chose to illustrate those particular events in the story? Which events would you have chosen to illustrate?

6. After distributing the Enrichment Activities sheet for *Julian's Glorious Summer*, ask the students to look carefully at the illustration and describe how the objects in this picture relate to the story.

RELATED BOOKS

Other books about Julian:
    Julian, Secret Agent. New York: Random House, 1988.
    More Stories Julian Tells. New York: Pantheon, 1981.
    The Stories Julian Tells. New York: Knopf, 1986.

Carrick, Carol. *Dark and Full of Secrets.* New York: Clarion, 1984.

Fenner, Carol. *The Skates of Uncle Richard.* New York: Random House, 1978.

Flournoy, Valerie. *The Twins Strike Back.* New York: Dial, 1980.

Merrill, Jean. *The Toothpaste Millionaire.* Boston: Houghton Mifflin, 1972.

Thomas, Ianthe. *Eliza's Daddy.* New York: Harcourt Brace Jovanovich, 1976.

Williams, Barbara. *Mitzi and the Terrible Tyrannosaurus Rex.* New York: E. P. Dutton, 1982.
    Other books in the Mitzi series:
        Mitzi and the Elephants, 1985.
        Mitzi and Frederick the Great, 1984.
        Mitzi's Honeymoon with Nana Potts, 1983.

Other books in the Stepping Stones series:
    Bulla, Clyde Robert. *The Chalk Box Kid.* New York: Random House, 1987.

    Etra, Jonathan, and Stephanie Spinner. *Aliens for Breakfast.* New York: Random House, 1988.

    Hooks, William H. *Pioneer Cat.* New York: Random House, 1988.

    Marzollo, Jean. *Red Ribbon Rosie.* New York: Random House, 1988.

    O'Connor, Jim, and Jane O'Connor. *The Ghost in Tent 19.* New York: Random House, 1988.

Saunders, Susan. *The Daring Rescue of Marlon the Swimming Pig.* New York: Random House, 1987.

Shreve, Susan. *Lily and the Runaway Baby.* New York: Random House, 1987.

Skurzynski, Gloria. *The Minstrel in the Tower.* New York: Random House, 1988.

Stevenson, Jocelyn. *O'Diddy.* New York: Random House, 1988.

Whelan, Gloria. *Next Spring an Oriole.* New York: Random House, 1987.

_____. *Silver.* New York: Random House, 1988.

Yep, Laurence. *The Curse of the Squirrel.* New York: Random House, 1987.

ENRICHMENT ACTIVITIES

Julian's Glorious Summer

1. The author of this book likes to use comparisons to give the reader a clearer picture of what the characters are feeling. For example, on page 18, Julian says, "I tried to sound braver than ever, like a spaceboy who had to be left behind on an asteroid." Make up other comparisons to show feelings.

   As brave as _____
   As lonely as _____
   As happy as _____
   As angry as _____
   As frightened as _____
   etc.

   Illustrate some of the most interesting comparisons. Be sure to write a caption for each picture you draw.

2. Interview several children and adults to find out how they learned to ride a bike. Be sure to include how old they were, whose bike they used, who helped them, and what happened. Share their stories with the class.

3. Design your ideal bike. Draw it and label the important parts.

4. Write a story about a time when you were afraid and what you did about it.

5. Ask 10 of your classmates what jobs they are expected to do at home and what, if any, rewards they get for doing these jobs. Chart the information you gather and share it with the group.

6. Bicycles have changed a great deal since they were first invented. Find out about some of the earlier bicycles. Draw pictures of several different kinds, and write a couple of sentences about each. Be sure to include where and when they were invented, what they were called, and how they were used.

7. Read another book about Julian:
   Julian, Secret Agent
   More Stories Julian Tells
   The Stories Julian Tells

8. Design your own activity for *Julian's Glorious Summer*.

Jumanji

Author: Chris Van Allsburg

Illustrator: Chris Van Allsburg

Publisher, Date: Houghton Mifflin, 1981

Pages: (not numbered)

SUMMARY

When their parents go out for the afternoon, Judy and Peter go to the park and find a mysterious game, "Jumanji: A Jungle Adventure Game." Once they begin to play they realize that each move leads to a *real* adventure and they must figure out how to survive until the end of the game.

PRE-READING/MOTIVATIONAL ACTIVITIES

1. Display a game board with a path or paths, markers, and dice (such as Uncle Wiggily or Winnie-the-Pooh). Make sure all of the children understand how these games are played.

2. Ask the students to read the title and look at the picture on the cover of the book. Ask them these questions:
    What do you think the story is going to be about?
    Who do you think the main characters are going to be?
    What do you think is the setting of the story?

3. Look at the first illustration of the book. Ask the children:
    What kind of story do you think this is going to be? Why?
    What does the picture suggest about the story?

VOCABULARY/DISCUSSION QUESTIONS

Vocabulary:

opera	stampede	horror
jungle	erupts	hunched
revealing	exhaustion	sleeping sickness
designed	slouched	mantel
absolute	protested	molten lava
monsoon season	restless	nudge
tsetse fly	casually	

Questions:

1. Why do you think Judy and Peter pick up the game, bring it home, and begin to play it even though it looked boring to them?

2. How are Judy and Peter alike? How are they different?

3. Why do you think the children and the guide don't speak to each other?

4. Why did the children play the game by the rules?

5. Are the dangers the children face real or imaginary?

6. Do you think the children could be hurt by the dangers they encounter?

7. Is Jumanji a dream come true or a nightmare?

8. Prediction: What do you think will happen to Danny and Walter?

9. Why do you think the author named the book and the game "Jumanji"?

10. Look at the illustrations. Now, imagine the illustrations are photographs. Where would the photographer have to stand to take the pictures? How do these unusual viewing angles contribute to the story?

11. Leader: Read other books by Chris Van Allsburg to the group. Point out recurring visual motifs (dogs, flowers, sailboats, etc.).

RELATED BOOKS

Van Allsburg, Chris. *Ben's Dream*. Boston: Houghton Mifflin, 1982.

_____ . *The Garden of Abdul Gasazi*. Boston: Houghton Mifflin, 1979.

_____ . *The Mysteries of Harris Burdick*. Boston: Houghton Mifflin, 1984.

_____ . *The Polar Express*. Boston: Houghton Mifflin, 1985.

_____ . *The Stranger*. Boston: Houghton Mifflin, 1986.

_____ . *Two Bad Ants*. Boston: Houghton Mifflin, 1988.

_____ . *The Wreck of the Zephyr*. Boston: Houghton Mifflin, 1983.

_____ . *The Z Was Zapped*. Boston: Houghton Mifflin, 1987.

ENRICHMENT ACTIVITIES

Jumanji

1. Make up a game with a game board similar to Jumanji, but with a different theme or habitat (an ocean adventure game, a desert adventure game, a Moon adventure game, etc.). Play it with your friends.

2. Write a sequel to *Jumanji*.

3. Watch a videotape of the movie *The Wizard of Oz*. Tell how the video and the story are alike and different.

4. Read other books by Chris Van Allsburg. How are they alike and different?

5. Make *Jumanji* into a play. Have one person narrate the story while others act it out. Allow the audience to use its imagination by using few props.

6. Draw a picture showing what the living room looked like just before the game was finished. Draw another picture of it after the game was over.

7. Create your own activity for *Jumanji*.

Nate the Great and the Fishy Prize

Author: Marjorie Weinman Sharmat

Illustrator: Marc Simont

Publisher, Date: Putnam, 1985

Pages: 48

SUMMARY

This is a detective story told in the first person by Nate the Great, detective extraordinaire. In this adventure Nate must find the missing gold-painted tuna can, which was to be first prize in Rosamond's Smartest Pet Contest.

PRE-READING/MOTIVATIONAL ACTIVITIES

1. Discuss: What is a detective? How do they solve crimes?

2. Play a memory game with the class. Ask four students, one at a time, to close their eyes and describe with as much detail as possible the attire of another classmate. Each student should describe a different classmate. The class can judge which one of the descriptions reveals the best memory for detail.

3. Ask the students to read the title and look at the picture on the cover of the book. Ask them these questions:
    What do you think the story is going to be about?
    Who do you think the main characters are going to be?
    What do you think is the setting of the story?

4. Read pages 7-12 of the story together. Ask the children to predict what happened to the prize. Make a list of their predictions and refer to it during discussions of the story.

VOCABULARY/DISCUSSION QUESTIONS

Vocabulary:

fishy (p. 14)
stampede (p. 18)
stumped (p. 38)

eel (p. 15)
swooshing (p. 33)
solve (p. 40)

26 / Nate the Great and the Fishy Prize

Questions:

1. Why do you think Nate is called "Nate the Great"?

2. What qualities does he have that make him a good detective?

3. What does Rosamond do that is strange?

4. Did you figure out the mystery before Nate the Great did? When did you know what happened to the prize?

5. Who do you think deserves credit for solving the mystery?

6. What parts of the story do you think are funny? Why?

7. Look at the book's illustrations. How does the artwork reflect the text? Why do you think the artist chose to illustrate those particular events in the story? Which events would you have chosen to illustrate?

RELATED BOOKS

Other books in the Nate the Great series:
Nate the Great, 1973.
Nate the Great and the Boring Beach Bag, 1987.
Nate the Great and the Lost List, 1975.
Nate the Great and the Missing Key, 1981.
Nate the Great and the Phony Clue, 1977.
Nate the Great and the Snowy Trail, 1982.
Nate the Great and the Sticky Case, 1978.
Nate the Great Goes Undercover, 1974.
Nate the Great Stalks Stupidweed, 1986.

Adler, David A. *Cam Jansen and the Mystery at the Monkey House*. New York: Viking Kestrel, 1985.
Other books in the Cam Jansen series:
Cam Jansen and the Mystery of the Babe Ruth Baseball, 1982.
Cam Jansen and the Mystery of the Carnival Prize, 1984.
Cam Jansen and the Mystery of the Dinosaur Bones, 1981.
Cam Jansen and the Mystery of the Gold Coins, 1982.
Cam Jansen and the Mystery of the Stolen Corn Popper, 1986.
Cam Jansen and the Mystery of the Stolen Diamonds, 1980.
Cam Jansen and the Mystery of the Television Dog, 1981.
Cam Jansen and the Mystery of the U.F.O., 1980.

Levy, Elizabeth. *Something Queer Is Going On*. New York: Delacorte, 1973.
Other books in the Something Queer series:
Something Queer at the Ball Park, 1975.

Something Queer at the Haunted School, 1982.
Something Queer at the Lemonade Stand, 1982.
Something Queer at the Library, 1977.
Something Queer in Rock 'n Roll, 1987.
Something Queer on Vacation, 1980.

Quackenbush, Robert. *Express Train to Trouble.* Englewood Cliffs, N.J.: Prentice-Hall, 1981.
Other Miss Mallard Mysteries:
Bicycle to Treachery, 1985.
Cable Car to Catastrophe, 1982.
Dig to Disaster, 1982.
Gondola to Danger, 1983.
Rickshaw to Horror, 1984.
Stagedoor to Terror, 1984.
Stairway to Doom, 1983.
Surfboard to Peril, 1986.
Taxi to Intrigue, 1984.
Texas Trail to Calamity, 1986.

ENRICHMENT ACTIVITIES

Nate the Great and the Fishy Prize

1. Find a recipe for pancakes and make them.

2. You are in charge of the prizes for the contest. Design a prize for each of the pets in the story.

3. Read other Nate the Great books.

4. Write another Nate the Great mystery.

5. Write *Nate the Great and the Fishy Prize* as a play. Act it out.

6. Ask someone from the humane society or a veterinarian to visit the class to discuss pets.

7. Interview someone who takes care of other people's pets for a living. Ask about some of the funny things that have happened to them.

8. Design your own activity for *Nate the Great and the Fishy Prize*.

Something Queer at the Library

Author: Elizabeth Levy

Illustrator: Mordicai Gerstein

Publisher, Date: Delacorte, 1977

Pages: (not numbered)

SUMMARY

Gwen and Jill enter Jill's basset hound, Fletcher, in a dog show. They go to the library to get books to help them train Fletcher, but to their dismay, they find pictures have been cut out of many of the books. The girls decide to track down the villain, and the trail leads right to the dog show.

PRE-READING/MOTIVATIONAL ACTIVITIES

1. Ask the students to read the title and look at the picture on the cover of the book. Ask them these questions:
   What do you think the story is going to be about?
   Who do you think the main characters are going to be?
   What do you think is the setting of the story?

2. Ask your school librarian to review book care with the students. Explain that library books are public property (belong to everyone), are expensive, and are purchased with tax money.

3. Discuss the characteristics of a good detective, for example, a good detective is smart, notices details, is persistent, thinks logically, is observant, is imaginative, and knows how to locate information.

4. If students are unfamiliar with dog shows, show them books like *Man's Best Friend* (published by the National Geographic Society) that contain pictures and information about dog shows.

VOCABULARY/DISCUSSION QUESTIONS

Vocabulary:

pure-bred	doodle	stacks (library shelving)
clue	captions	Irish setters
margin	encyclopedia	Airedales

(vocabulary list continues on next page)

30 / Something Queer at the Library

accused	braces	lopsided whatchamacallits
congratulations	gait	Old English sheepdogs
basset hound	Lhasa apso	fox terriers
fingerprint	Tibet	loudspeaker

Questions:

1. Why do you think Mr. Hobart let the girls take the books out?

2. Why do the girls think Mr. Hobart will assume they cut the pictures out of the books?

3. List the clues in the order they are found. Then, list the clues in the order of their importance to the case. Explain why some clues are more important than others.

4. Do you think Pam's parents were reasonable about not letting her get books about dogs? Explain.

5. Are Gwen and Jill a good team? Explain.

6. What are Fletcher's strengths? What is his role in solving the mystery?

7. Look at the book's illustrations. How does the artwork reflect the text? Why do you think the artist chose to illustrate those particular events in the story? Which events would you have chosen to illustrate?

RELATED BOOKS

Other Something Queer books:
Something Queer at the Ball Park, 1975.
Something Queer at the Haunted School, 1982.
Something Queer at the Lemonade Stand, 1982.
Something Queer in Rock 'n Roll, 1987.
Something Queer Is Going On, 1973.
Something Queer on Vacation, 1980.

Fox, Michael, and Wende Devlin Gates. *What Is Your Dog Saying?* New York: Coward, McCann & Geoghegan, 1977.

Fujimoto, Patricia. *Libraries.* Chicago: Children's Press, 1984.

Landshoff, Ursula. *Okay, Good Dog.* New York: Harper & Row, 1978.

Levy, Elizabeth. *Dracula Is a Pain in the Neck.* New York: Harper & Row, 1983.

_____. *Frankenstein Moved in on the Fourth Floor.* New York: Harper & Row, 1979.

_____. *Lizzie Lies a Lot.* New York: Delacorte, 1976.

_____. *Nice Little Girls.* New York: Delacorte, 1974.

_____. *The Shadow Nose.* New York: Morrow, 1983.

National Geographic Society. *Man's Best Friend.* Washington, D.C.: National Geographic Society, 1966.

Quackenbush, Robert. *Express Train to Trouble.* Englewood Cliffs, N.J.: Prentice-Hall, 1981.
    Other Miss Mallard Mysteries:
        Bicycle to Treachery, 1985.
        Cable Car to Catastrophe, 1982.
        Dig to Disaster, 1982.
        Gondola to Danger, 1983.
        Rickshaw to Horror, 1984.
        Stagedoor to Terror, 1984.
        Stairway to Doom, 1983.
        Surfboard to Peril, 1986.
        Taxi to Intrigue, 1984.
        Texas Trail to Calamity, 1986.

Sabin, Louis. *All about Dogs as Pets.* New York: Julian Messner, 1983.

ENRICHMENT ACTIVITIES

Something Queer at the Library

1. What is your favorite breed of dog? You may want to look in a dog book to help you decide. Make a poster that gives information about the breed, including appearance, characteristics, and history.

2. Write an original Something Queer story.

3. Read another Something Queer story. Make a chart comparing the story to *Something Queer at the Library*. Be sure to include how the books are alike and how they are different.

4. Make a three-dimensional model of Fletcher.

5. Write a new ending to the story, making the chocolate-eating boy the "creep."

6. Make a map of the layout of the dog show. Use a dotted line to show the characters' routes during the chase.

7. Make a fact card file of information about Tibet, home of the Lhasa apso. Write each thing you learn about Tibet on a separate card. Share your most interesting facts with the group.

8. Rewrite the story as a play. Perform it for the group.

9. Read a mystery by another author.

10. Create your own activity for *Something Queer at the Library*.

Wagon Wheels

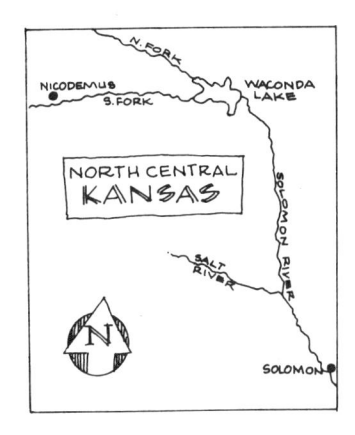

Author: Barbara Brenner

Illustrator: Don Bolognese

Publisher, Date: Harper & Row, 1978

Pages: 64

SUMMARY

After the Civil War, the Muldie family journeys to Nicodemus, Kan., where black families can homestead their own land. They face blizzards, famine, and prairie fires. They are helped by people in the community and Osage Indians who live nearby.

PRE-READING/MOTIVATIONAL ACTIVITIES

1. Locate Nicodemus, Kan., where the story begins, on a map of the central United States. As the story of the Muldie family unfolds, refer back to the map to locate the Solomon River and Solomon City, Kan.

2. To help students understand the historical setting of the story, briefly discuss the following topics: slavery, the Civil War, the Emancipation Proclamation, the Homestead Act, and pioneers. *See* Related Books for some sources.

3. Show students pictures of the prairie and a dugout (*see* Related Books). Discuss why people lived in this kind of house.

4. Ask the students to read the title and look at the picture on the cover of the book. Ask them these questions:
    What do you think the story is going to be about?
    Who do you think the main characters are going to be?
    What do you think is the setting of the story?

VOCABULARY/DISCUSSION QUESTIONS

Chapters 1-2:

Vocabulary:

Nicodemus, Kansas (p. 7)
prairie (p. 11)
dugout (p. 13)
cornmeal mush (p. 19)
saddlebag (p. 24)

Kentucky (p. 8)
carpenter (p. 11)
banjo (p. 16)
supply train (p. 21)
Osage Indians (p. 29)

Questions:

1. What are the bad things about living in a dugout? What are the good things?

2. Why do you think the boys didn't complain much about the hardships in their lives?

3. Why do you think the people of Nicodemus did not shoot at the Indians when they rode "straight toward the dugouts"? (p. 25)

4. Why do you think the Indians gave the settlers food and firewood?

5. Why do you think Daddy made a point of telling the boys what to say when someone says bad things about Indians?

Chapters 3-4:

Vocabulary:

shelter (p. 30)
"off his head" (p. 34)
post rider (p. 44)
deer trail (p. 46)
panthers (p. 51)
rattlesnake (p. 53)

molasses (p. 33)
prairie fire (p. 39)
Solomon City (p. 46)
wolves (p. 51)
coyotes (p. 51)

Questions:

1. Why doesn't Daddy take the boys with him when he leaves?

2. On page 32 Johnny says he is afraid to be left alone. Why does he later tell Mrs. Sadler and Mrs. Hickman that he and his brothers can take care of themselves? (p. 34)

3. Why do you think Daddy was so sure that the boys could make the 150-mile journey to Solomon City? (p. 47)

4. Review the difficulties the boys faced in making the journey (following the map, staying awake at night, wild animals, the long walk, etc.). Which do you think was the most difficult? Why?

5. Why is *Wagon Wheels* a good title for this book?

6. Look at the book's illustrations. How does the artwork reflect the text? Why do you think the artist chose to illustrate those particular events in the story? Which events would you have chosen to illustrate?

7. One read-aloud book that complements *Wagon Wheels* is *Little House on the Prairie*, by Laura Ingalls Wilder. Compare the two books, considering the setting, dangers faced and overcome, and attitudes toward Indians.

RELATED BOOKS

Aliki. *A Weed Is a Flower: The Life of George Washington Carver*. Englewood Cliffs, N.J.: Prentice-Hall, 1965.

Benchley, Nathaniel. *George the Drummer Boy*. New York: Harper & Row, 1977.

_____. *Sam the Minuteman*. New York: Harper & Row, 1969.

_____. *Small Wolf*. New York: Harper & Row, 1972.

Chace, G. Earl. *Wonders of Rattlesnakes*. New York: Dodd, Mead, 1975.

Durham, Philip, and Everett L. Jones. *The Adventures of the Negro Cowboys*. New York: Dodd, Mead, 1965.

Fradin, Dennis B. *Pioneers*. A New True Book. Chicago: Children's Press, 1984.

Freedman, Russell. *Children of the Wild West*. New York: Clarion/Houghton Mifflin, 1983.

_____. *Rattlesnakes*. New York: Holiday House, 1984.

Greenfield, Eloise. *Mary McLeod Bethune*. New York: Crowell, 1977.

Katz, William Loren. *An Album of the Civil War*. New York: Watts, 1974.

Meriwether, Louise. *The Heart Man: Dr. Daniel Hale Williams*. Englewood Cliffs, N.J.: Prentice-Hall, 1972.

Monjo, F. N. *The Drinking Gourd*. New York: Harper & Row, 1970.

_____. *Indian Summer*. New York: Harper & Row, 1968.

Rowan, James P. *Prairies and Grasslands*. A New True Book. Chicago: Children's Press, 1983.

Walker, Barbara Muhs. *The Little House Cookbook: Frontier Food from Laura Ingalls Wilder's Classic Stories.* New York: Harper & Row, 1979.

Wilder, Laura Ingalls. *Little House on the Prairie.* New York: Harper & Row, 1953.

Wilson, Terry P. *The Osage.* New York: Chelsea House, 1988.

Wise, William. *Booker T. Washington.* New York: Putnam, 1968.

ENRICHMENT ACTIVITIES

Wagon Wheels

1. Find a recipe for cornmeal mush and prepare it for the class.

2. Find out more about the Osage Indians. Draw pictures showing interesting things about their way of life at the time of the story. Write captions for your pictures.

3. Find out about the weather in Kansas. Make a graph that compares the summer and winter temperatures.

4. Make a diorama or mural showing the animal and plant life of the prairie.

5. Read a book about rattlesnakes. Make a fact card file by writing each thing you learn about them on a separate card. Share your most interesting facts with the group.

6. Find out more about mail service in the 1870s. Share what you learn with the class.

7. Make a map that shows the journey of the Muldie family. Be sure to include Kentucky; Nicodemus, Kan.; Solomon City, Kan.; the Solomon River; and the deer trail.

8. Write a letter that Johnny might have written to the people in Nicodemus about the boys' journey to Solomon City.

9. Read a biography of a famous black American who lived during the time this book takes place (for example, George Washington Carver, Booker T. Washington, Mary McLeod Bethune). What were their experiences in the years following the Civil War?

10. Design your own activity for *Wagon Wheels*.

GRADE THREE

Altogether, One at a Time

Author: E. L. Konigsburg

Illustrators: Gail E. Haley, Mercer Mayer, Gary Parker, Laurel Schindelman

Publisher, Date: Aladdin/Atheneum, 1971

Pages: 79

SUMMARY

The book contains four short stories narrated by four very different children and illustrated by four different artists. Each deals with a moment of understanding in that child's life.

PRE-READING/MOTIVATIONAL ACTIVITIES

"Inviting Jason"

1. Discuss with the students the kinds of things they consider when inviting kids to their birthday parties. How do these things change as they get older?

2. Discuss times when the students have *had* to play with or entertain someone they didn't choose to play with. What happened?

3. With students, look up dyslexia in the dictionary. Discuss what it means. Some people have a difficult time reading because the message they see doesn't get from their eyes to their brains in the right way. Ask students to try reading a page of print upside-down or looking in a mirror. Did it take them a longer time to read? Was it more difficult to understand what they read?

"Night of the Leonids"

1. Ask students to look up *meteorite* and *meteorite shower* in a dictionary or encyclopedia.

2. Ask students who are close to their grandparents or other older adults to describe the kinds of things they do together.

40 / Altogether, One at a Time

"Camp Fat"

1. Ask students who have been to camp to describe their experiences. (What kind of camp was it? Did you enjoy yourself? Why or why not?)

2. Discuss students' problems or bad habits that bother their parents. What kinds of things have they done to try to solve the problem or break the habit? Have they worked?

"Momma at the Pearly Gates"

1. Discuss busing and segregated schools.

2. Discuss racial name calling. Why do people do it and why is it hurtful?

VOCABULARY/DISCUSSION QUESTIONS

"Inviting Jason"

Vocabulary:

decade (p. 2)	sarcastic (p. 3)
abbreviated (p. 3)	exclamation (p. 3)
dyslexia (p. 4)	contagious (p. 4)
faulty (p. 4)	tutored (p. 5)
boulevard (p. 5)	gentleman (p. 6)
concentration (p. 6)	measly (p. 8)
enthusiastic (p. 10)	

Questions:

1. Read the last three paragraphs of the story. How would Stanley's reasons for not wanting Jason at the party be "different" after the party than before the party?

"The Night of the Leonids"

Vocabulary:

go abroad (p. 15)	Eiffel (p. 16)
Coliseum (p. 16)	gin rummy (p. 17)
share and share alike (p. 18)	mugging (p. 19)
environment (p. 20)	

Altogether, One at a Time / 41

Questions:

1. What did Lewis mean when he said, "Sixty-three and thirty-three don't add up to another chance"? (p. 28)

2. Why did Lewis and his grandmother hold hands on the way back to her apartment at the end of the story?

"Camp Fat"

Vocabulary:

commercial (p. 31)
counsellors (p. 32)
indecent (p. 32)
glandular imbalance (p. 34)
convulsion (p. 38)
arthritis (p. 40)
celluloid (p. 45)

weigh-in (p. 31)
muscular (p. 32)
dialogue (p. 33)
Communists (p. 36)
tax deductible (p. 39)
exterior (p. 45)

Questions:

1. Who or what was Miss Natasha?

2. Read the last paragraph of the story. Why wouldn't Clara *need* to return to Camp Fat?

"Momma at the Pearly Gates"

Vocabulary:

got bused (p. 62)
transistors (p. 63)
fresh (attitude) (p. 77)

appreciated (p. 63)
imitating (p. 74)
credit (p. 78)

Questions:

1. Read the last three paragraphs of the story. What *was* "the other thing it was the beginning of"?

Questions about the book in general:

1. Look at each story's illustrations. How does the artwork in each reflect the text? Why do you think the artists chose to illustrate those particular events in each story? Which events would you have chosen to illustrate?

2. Now look at each picture on the Enrichment Activities page. How does each picture relate to its story?

RELATED BOOKS

Berger, Melvin. *Comets, Meteors and Asteroids*. New York: Putnam, 1981.

Bolliger, Max. *Noah and the Rainbow*. New York: Crowell, 1972.

Branley, Franklyn. *Comets, Meteroids, and Asteroids: Mavericks of the Solar System*. New York: Crowell, 1974.

Burns, Marilyn. *Good For Me! All about Food in 32 Bites*. Boston: Little, Brown, 1978.

Cohen, Daniel. *Real Ghosts*. New York: Dodd, Mead, 1977.

Darling, David J. *Comets, Meteors, and Asteroids*. Minneapolis, Minn.: Dillon Press, 1984.

Elborn, Andrew, and Ivan Gantschev. *Noah & the Ark & the Animals*. Natick, Mass.: Picture Book Studio USA, 1984.

Forrai, Maria S. *A Look at Prejudice and Understanding*. Minneapolis, Minn.: Lerner, 1976.

Hoffman, Betsy. *Haunted Places*. New York: Julian Messner, 1982.

Knight, David. *Meteors and Meteorites*. New York: Watts, 1969.

Konigsburg, E.L. *About the B'nai Bagels*. New York: Atheneum, 1969.

———. *The Dragon in the Ghetto Caper*. New York: Atheneum, 1974.

———. *From the Mixed-Up Files of Mrs. Basil E. Frankweiler*. New York: Atheneum, 1967.

———. *(George)*. New York: Atheneum, 1970.

———. *Jennifer, Hecate, Macbeth, William McKinley, and Me, Elizabeth*. New York: Atheneum, 1967.

———. *A Proud Taste for Scarlet and Miniver*. New York: Atheneum, 1973.

———. *The Second Mrs. Giaconda*. New York: Atheneum, 1975.

———. *Throwing Shadows*. New York: Atheneum, 1979.

Marek, Margot. *Different, Not Dumb*. New York: Watts, 1985.

Savage, John F. *Dyslexia: Understanding Reading Problems*. New York: Julian Messner, 1985.

Spier, Peter. *Noah's Ark*. Garden City, N.Y.: Doubleday, 1977.

Thompson, Paul. *Nutrition*. New York: Watts, 1981.

Waber, Bernard. *Ira Sleeps Over*. Boston, Houghton Mifflin, 1972.

ENRICHMENT ACTIVITIES

All Together, One at a Time

"Inviting Jason"

1. Find out more about dyslexia. Summarize what you find out for the group.
2. Read (or reread) *Ira Sleeps Over* by Bernard Waber. Make a chart that shows how the stories are similar and different.
3. Create your own activity for "Inviting Jason."

"Night of the Leonids"

1. What is a lifetime? Can you think of things that happen only once or twice in a lifetime? Make a list.
2. Make a fact card file on meteorites and meteorite showers. Write each thing you learn on a separate card. Share the most interesting facts with the group.
3. Create your own activity for "Night of the Leonids."

"Camp Fat"

1. Find a library book about the jewelry of Faberge or other antique European jewelry. Share the pictures with the group.
2. Find out about calories (*see* Related Books). Bring in fifty calories' worth of several different foods, such as chocolate, peanuts, celery, breakfast cereal, or raisins.
3. Some people would say that Miss Natasha was a ghost or spirit. Find out more about this phenomenon. Share this information with the class.
4. Create your own activity for "Camp Fat."

"Momma at the Pearly Gates"

1. Momma drew her version of Noah's Ark. Read a version of the story of Noah and the ark and draw your own ark.
2. Interview your parents about what school was like when they were your age. Find out what they wore, what games they played, what they studied, and what their teachers and classrooms were like. Take notes so that you can share the information with the group.
3. What kinds of talents or interests do you have that might develop into a lifelong hobby or occupation? Share your talent or interest with the group and explain how this might lead to an adult hobby or occupation.
4. Create your own activity for "Momma at the Pearly Gates."

The Celery Stalks at Midnight

Author: James Howe

Illustrator: Leslie Morrill

Publisher, Date: Atheneum, 1983

Pages: 111

SUMMARY

Harold the dog, Chester the cat, and their new friend, Howie the puppy, search for the missing vampire rabbit, Bunnicula. Harold describes their mishaps and adventures, which include a trip in a garbage truck with anemic vegetables and an encounter with children whom the animals suspect of turning into vampires. This book is a sequel to *Bunnicula* and *Howliday Inn* (see Related Books).

PRE-READING/MOTIVATIONAL ACTIVITIES

1. Read a book about vampires (for example, *Meet the Vampire* by Georgess McHargue).
   List the characteristics of a vampire:
   They suck blood.
   You can kill one by pounding a wooden stake through its heart.
   Garlic will keep one away.
   A person who is bitten by a vampire will become the vampire's slave.

2. Explain that a pun is:
   a. replacing one word with another that has a similar sound but a different meaning. ("A vampire," I explained, "is a person who calls the rules during a baseball game." (p. 7))
   b. a play on words using a double meaning. ("To my father, who raised me on a diet of corn, ham, and punster cheese." (dedication))

3. Ask the students if any of them have read the prequels to *The Celery Stalks at Midnight: Bunnicula* or *Howliday Inn*. Have them share what they know about the main characters from the earlier books.
   Or:
   Read *Bunnicula* to the group. Talk about puns and vampire characteristics as you read the story.

4. Tell the group that the story is being told by a dog named Harold who likes to use "big words." Encourage them to use context as much as possible to help them figure out the meanings of these unknown words. Explain that Harold is telling the story as a flashback: something that has already happened.

5. Ask the students to read the title and look at the picture on the cover of the book. Ask them these questions:
   What do you think the story is going to be about?
   Who do you think the main characters are going to be?
   What do you think is the setting of the story?

VOCABULARY/DISCUSSION QUESTIONS

Introduction—Chapter 2:

Vocabulary:

publishing business (p. ix)
receipt (p. ix)
latter (p. x)
harrowing (p. xi)
domesticated (p. 6)
skulked (p. 12)
hearken (p. 17)
delectable (p. 24)
zombie (p. 29)
dolt (p. 30)
fangs (p. 30)

literary agent (p. ix)
manuscript (p. ix)
bedraggled (p. xi)
elements (p. 3)
seamier (p. 7)
enterprise (p. 14)
badgering (p. 22)
aroma (p. 24)
minions (p. 29)
cowering (p. 30)
bickering (p. 32)

Questions:

1. Why does Harold sign his name Harold X? What does the "X" stand for?

2. Describe the main characters: Chester, Harold, Howie, and Bunnicula.

3. Why does the story begin, "It was *not* a dark and stormy night."?

4. Why do you think Chester is so intent on "getting" Bunnicula?

5. Why is Harold always so insistent that Bunnicula has done nothing wrong? What is Howie's role in the story?

Chapters 3-5:

Vocabulary:

destiny (p. 39)
chewing the fat (p. 45)
helter-skelter (p. 54)
cascaded (p. 62)
heart palpitations (p. 64)

hors d'oeuvres (p. 41)
haunches (p. 50)
error of judgement (p. 57)
toupee (p. 63)
champing at the bit (p. 64)

(vocabulary continues on next page)

46 / The Celery Stalks at Midnight

adorned (p. 66)
nauseated (p. 67)
various specimens
　of vegetable specters (p. 68)
strewn (p. 66)
repast (p. 68)
culprits (p. 70)
invigorates (p. 77)

Questions:

1. Read the last sentence on page 71. What does this tell you about Chester's character?

2. What does Howie mean when he says, "I'm too me to die." (p. 72)

3. What do you think has happened to Bunnicula? Why are the vegetables white? Write your predictions on a piece of paper.

Chapters 6-8:

Vocabulary:

stealthing (p. 79)
scrumptious (p. 98)
Rubik's Cube (p. 104)
drastic (p. 85)
semblance of normalcy (p. 103)
prey (p. 108)

Questions:

1. Read the last three paragraphs on page 41. At this point Harold seems unconcerned about vampires. When does Harold really become convinced that they have vampire problems?

2. Chester describes what has happened as "a slight misinterpretation of the facts." Compare what the animals think is happening at the school fair to what is really happening.

3. Why is it so easy for the animals to jump to conclusions about what Toby and Pete are doing?

4. What is the thump . . . thump . . . thump at the end of the story?

5. Do you think Bunnicula is a vampire? Support your answer.

6. Look at the book's illustrations. How does the artwork reflect the text? Why do you think the artist chose to illustrate those particular events in the story? Which events would you have chosen to illustrate?

RELATED BOOKS

Other books in the Bunnicula series:
　Bunnicula, 1979.
　Howliday Inn, 1982.
　Nighty-nightmare, 1987.

Aylesworth, Thomas G. *The Story of Vampires.* New York: McGraw-Hill, 1977.

———. *Vampires and Other Ghosts.* New York: Addison-Wesley, 1972.

Bave, Colleen Stanley. *Rabbits and Hares.* New York: Dodd, Mead, 1983.

Doty, Roy. *Puns, Gags, Quips and Riddles.* Garden City, N.Y.: Doubleday, 1974.

Howe, James. *Eat Your Poison, Dear: A Sebastian Barth Mystery.* New York: Atheneum, 1986.

———. *Morgan's Zoo.* New York: Atheneum, 1984.

———. *Stage Fright: A Sebastian Barth Mystery.* New York: Atheneum, 1986.

———. *What Eric Knew: A Sebastian Barth Mystery.* New York: Atheneum, 1985.

Keller, Charles. *Punch Lines.* Englewood Cliffs, N.J.: Prentice-Hall, 1975.

Levy, Elizabeth. *Dracula Is a Pain in the Neck.* New York: Harper & Row, 1983.

———. *Frankenstein Moved in on the Fourth Floor.* New York: Harper & Row, 1979.

McHargue, Georgess. *Meet the Vampire.* New York: Lippincott, 1979.

Phillips, Louis. *How Do You Get a Horse out of the Bathtub?* New York: Viking, 1983.

Pinkwater, Daniel Manus. *Attack of Attila the Pun.* New York: Four Winds, 1981.

———. *The Moosepire.* Boston: Little, Brown, 1986.

Pope, Joyce. *Taking Care of Your Rabbit.* New York: Watts, 1987.

Silverstein, Alvin. *Rabbits: All about Them.* New York: Lothrop, Lee & Shepard, 1973.

Zim, Herbert S. *Rabbits.* New York: Morrow, 1948.

ENRICHMENT ACTIVITIES

The Celery Stalks at Midnight

1. Do a scientific experiment to find out if vegetables can be turned white. Try several different methods. Use the Scientific Experiment Worksheet on page 49 to record your experiment. Report your results to the group.

2. Interview people who have had rabbits as pets. Find out of their rabbits ever got out of their cages. Were there any unexplained escapes? Report your findings to the group.

3. Survey at least 10 people to find out if they believe in vampires. Ask them to explain why or why not. Compile your results and share them with the group.

4. Many of the scenes in the book would make good one-act plays. Choose one of these scenes, rewrite it in play form, and perform it for the group. Be sure to let your audience know that this is an excerpt from a book and that they can find out more about these characters by reading *The Celery Stalks at Midnight*.

5. Make puppets of the characters Howie, Harold, Chester, and Bunnicula. Create a play for them. The play could be a scene from the book or a scene you make up in which the characters act like themselves.

6. There are very few pictures of Bunnicula. Draw a picture of him. Make a "Wanted" poster for Bunnicula, listing the bunny's "crimes" from Chester's point of view.

7. Make a fact card file on vampires. Write one fact about vampires on each card. Share your cards with the group.

8. Make a poster that explains what a pun is. Use puns from the book or others that you like as examples.

9. On pages 80-84 the animals are watching a performance of Toby and Pete's play, *Curse of the Vampires,* but they leave before the end. What happens after Pete shouts, "On to Castle Bunnicula!"? Write the script for their play, including your own version of the play's conclusion. Perform it for the group.

10. Create your own activity for *The Celery Stalks at Midnight*.

SCIENTIFIC EXPERIMENT WORKSHEET

Statement of the Problem: How can vegetables be turned white?

Procedure: (What to do?)	Materials: (What do you need?)	Data: (What happened?)	Results: (Did this work?)

Conclusion: What method worked best?

The Celery Stalks at Midnight / 49

The Hundred Dresses

Author: Eleanor Estes

Illustrator: Louis Slobodkin

Publisher, Date: Harcourt Brace Jovanovich/Scholastic, 1944

Pages: 79

SUMMARY

Wanda Petronski, who lives in a poor section of town, is ignored by her classmates until the day she tells them that she owns 100 dresses. Then the teasing starts. Eventually the children discover that there is more to Wanda than they had thought, but it is too late to make amends. This is a story about the destructive power of prejudice.

PRE-READING/MOTIVATIONAL ACTIVITIES

1. Discuss immigration. Ask the students: What is immigration? Why do people leave their homelands? What would it be like to move to a country where no one spoke your language and the customs were unfamiliar to you? What do you think might happen to you?

2. The original copyright date of this book is 1944. Discuss how schools might have been different in the 1930s and 1940s than they are today. Students could interview older adults about their elementary school experiences. What type of rules did they have? How did the children behave? What was the teacher's role in school? In what ways have schools stayed the same? How are schools different now?

3. Ask the students to read the title and look at the picture on the cover of the book. Ask them these questions:
    What do you think the story is going to be about?
    Who do you think the main characters are going to be?
    What do you think is the setting of the story?

VOCABULARY/DISCUSSION QUESTIONS

Chapters 1-2:

Vocabulary:

    reciting in unison (p. 6)   Gettysburg Address (p. 6)
    incredulous (p. 15)   sapolio (p. 19)

Questions:

1. What was Wanda Petronski's relationship with her classmates? Why do you think the children made fun of her sometimes and didn't notice her at other times?

2. Why did Peggy tease Wanda?

3. Why did Maddie go along with it?

4. How do you think the teacher felt about Wanda?

Chapters 3-4:

Vocabulary:

crimson (p. 21)
absent-mindedly (p. 24)
cerise-colored (p. 38)

daily dozen (p. 22)
looked stolidly (p. 31)

Questions:

1. Chapter 3 is a flashback to a time before the story takes place. Why does the author use the flashback in this chapter?

2. How had the teasing begun?

3. Reread p. 33. Why do you think Peggy was so interested in teasing Wanda?

4. Reread p. 35. Why do you think Maddie didn't tell Peggy to stop? Why did she tear up the note?

5. Why do you think Wanda insisted that she had 100 dresses?

6. Prediction: Maddie is feeling guilty because she has been teasing Wanda about the dresses. What do you think she will do? Explain your prediction.

Chapters 5-7:

Vocabulary:

exquisite (p. 45)
assailed (p. 52)
unintelligible (p. 60)

foreigner (p. 52)
make amends (p. 57)
disconsolate (p. 61)

52 / The Hundred Dresses

Questions:

1. Reread Mr. Petronski's letter on page 46. Why was his family moving? What did he mean when he said, "No more holler Polack"?

2. How did his letter affect the people in the class?

3. Why did Maddie have "a very sick feeling in the bottom of her stomach"? (p. 47)

4. Why do you think Maddie was so eager to make amends?

5. How did Peggy try to justify her teasing of Wanda about the dresses?

6. Why was Maddie finally able to go to sleep?

7. How do you think Wanda's moving away will change Maddie's life?

8. How did Wanda's letter make the girls feel? Why didn't Maddie feel as relieved as Peggy?

9. Why was Maddie so relieved when Peggy wanted to go over to Wanda's house?

10. Do you agree that Wanda really "liked" Peggy and Maddie? Why or why not?

Questions about the book in general:

1. Why do you think the author began the story with the end?

2. When do you think Wanda began drawing her 100 dresses? Before she began being teased? After she was teased? When the contest was announced?

3. This story is realistic fiction. The events in this story could have happened in real life. If this story happened in the author's life, who do you think she was in the story? Explain your answer.

4. Role play the scene on pages 22-33, which takes place on the day that the 100 dresses game started. Why did Peggy start the game? Why do you think everyone else went along with it?

5. Look at the book's illustrations. How does the artwork reflect the text? Why do you think the artist chose to illustrate those particular events in the story? Which events would you have chosen to illustrate?

RELATED BOOKS

Blumenthal, Shirley. *Coming to America: Immigrants from Eastern Europe.* New York: Delacorte, 1981.

Cohen, Barbara. *Goosebeeries to Oranges.* New York: Lothrop, Lee & Shepard, 1982.

_____. *Molly's Pilgrim.* New York: Lothrop, Lee & Shepard, 1983.

Estes, Eleanor. *The Alley.* New York: Harcourt Brace & World, 1964.

_____. *The Coat-Hanger Christmas Tree.* New York: Atheneum, 1973.

_____. *The Curious Adventures of Jimmy McGee.* New York: Harcourt Brace Jovanovich, 1987.

_____. *Ginger Pye.* New York: Harcourt Brace, 1951.

_____. *The Lost Umbrella of Kim Chu.* New York: Atheneum, 1978.

_____. *The Middle Moffat.* New York: Harcourt, 1942.

_____. *Miranda the Great.* New York: Harcourt Brace & World, 1967.

_____. *The Moffat Museum.* New York: Harcourt Brace Jovanovich, 1983.

_____. *The Moffats.* New York: Harcourt, 1941.

_____. *Pinky Pye.* New York: Harcourt, 1958.

_____. *Rufus M.* New York: Harcourt, 1943.

_____. *The Tunnel of Hugsy Goode.* New York: Harcourt Brace Jovanovich, 1972.

_____. *The Witch Family.* New York: Harcourt, 1960.

Fisher, Leonard Everett. *Ellis Island: Gateway to the New World.* New York: Holiday House, 1986.

Freedman, Russell. *Immigrant Kids.* New York: E. P. Dutton, 1980.

Heller, Linda. *The Castle on Hester Street.* Philadelphia: Jewish Publication Society of America, 1982.

Sandin, Joan. *The Long Way to a New Land.* New York: Harper & Row, 1981.

Waterton, Betty. *Pettranella.* New York: Vanguard, 1980.

Wytrwal, Joseph Anthony. *The Poles in America.* Minneapolis, Minn.: Lerner, 1969.

Picture Sets:

Immigration. Mt. Dora, Fla.: Documentary Photo Aids.

ENRICHMENT ACTIVITIES

The Hundred Dresses

1. Talk to your parents about your ethnic heritage. When did your ancestors come to this country? Why did they come here? Take notes so you can share the information with the group.

2. Wanda came from Poland. Find out about the arts and crafts of Poland. Create something to share with the group that shows what you have learned.

3. Look up *discrimination, prejudice, name-calling,* and *slur* in a dictionary. Explain in your own words what these words mean. Give examples of each from the story.

4. Have a fashion-drawing contest. Ask someone not in the contest to be the judge. After the contest, discuss how it feels to be the winner and the loser.

5. Write a letter from Maddie to Wanda in which Maddie explains why she treated Wanda the way she did.

6. The scene that describes how the teasing began is on pages 22-33. Rewrite this scene as a play, and ask some group members to help you perform it for the rest of the group.

7. The class in the story recited the Gettysburg Address every morning. Look up the Gettysburg Address in an encyclopedia. Find out who wrote it and why it was written. If possible, make copies of it and ask the other members of the group to recite it with you.

8. Read another book by Eleanor Estes.

9. Create your own activity for *The Hundred Dresses*.

On the Banks of Plum Creek

Author: Laura Ingalls Wilder

Illustrator: Garth Williams

Publisher, Date: Harper & Row, 1953

Pages: 339

SUMMARY

The Ingalls family moves from Kansas to Minnesota and settles in a dugout on the banks of Plum Creek. Laura and Mary attend school for the first time, the family faces hardship when a plague of grasshoppers eats their wheat crop, and Pa must leave the family to find work. This book is the sequel to *Little House on the Prairie*.

PRE-READING/MOTIVATIONAL ACTIVITIES

1. Read chapters 25 ("Soldiers") and 26 ("Going Out") of *Little House on the Prairie* aloud to the group to set the scene for *On the Banks of Plum Creek*. *On the Banks of Plum Creek* is the third in the series of Laura Ingalls Wilder's Little House books, coming after *Little House on the Prairie*.

2. Ask the students to read the title and look at the picture on the cover of the book. Ask them these questions:
    What do you think the story is going to be about?
    Who do you think the main characters are going to be?
    What do you think is the setting of the story?

3. Look at a map of the central United States and trace the family's journey before this book begins. Locate the Verdigris River (close to Coffeyville, Kan.). This is where the Ingalls' journey to Minnesota began. At the beginning of *On the Banks of Plum Creek* the family had come "all the way from the little log house in Indian Territory, across Kansas, across Missouri, across Iowa, and a long way into Minnesota." The end of their journey was Walnut Grove, Minn. (near Marshall).

56 / On the Banks of Plum Creek

4. As you read the book, you may want to show students pictures of the prairie, prairie plants and animals, dugout houses, and sod houses.

Note: There are several ways to approach the reading of this book. One, of course, is to have each student read the entire book independently. For a book of this length, an equally effective technique might be to combine reading aloud to the group by the group leader with independent student reading.

VOCABULARY/DISCUSSION QUESTIONS

Chapters 1-7:

Vocabulary:

prairie (p. 1)	Indian Territory (p. 1)
mustangs (p. 3)	slunk (p. 4)
picket-lines (p. 5)	Norwegians (p. 6)
dugout (p. 6)	Half-pint (p. 7)
Indian ponies (p. 7)	oxen (p. 7)
wagon bows (p. 8)	morning-glory (p. 10)
whitewashed (p. 10)	greased-paper (p. 10)
sod (p. 11)	bedsteads (p. 14)
manger (p. 15)	blue flags (flower) (p. 19)
rushes (p. 20)	sunbonnet (p. 22)
plum thickets (p. 22)	tableland (p. 22)
calico (p. 23)	black-eyed Susans (p. 28)
goldenrod (p. 28)	smothery (p. 29)
fiddle (p. 32)	badger (p. 34)
lichens (p. 37)	wreath (p. 40)
milch cow (p. 41)	chewing her cud (p. 41)
dewy (p. 45)	
steer (p. 50)	

Questions:

1. Why did the Ingalls decide to settle in Minnesota?

2. Why do you think Ma doesn't want to move right into the dugout? (p. 8)

3. Pa teaches Laura a lesson about wading in deep water by grabbing her foot and scaring her. Do you think that this is a good way of teaching Laura to obey? Explain.

4. Why does Laura disobey Pa by going back to the swimming-hole alone?

5. Why does Laura tell Pa what she has done even though he would never have found out about it?

6. Why does the punishment of having to stay at home with Ma work when scaring Laura did not?

7. Read page 44. Who do you think Pa considers "our kind of folks"?

8. Why does Ma rename the cow Spot instead of Wreath of Roses?

9. In chapter 7 ("Ox on the Roof") Laura and Mary are frightened by the cattle herd. "Mary was so scared that she could not move. Laura was so scared that she jumped right off the rock. She knew she had to drive Spot and Pete and Bright into the stable." (p. 47) What does this show about each of them?

Chapters 8-15:

Vocabulary:

scythe (p. 52)
plough (p. 53)
threshing-machine (p. 53)
wheat kernels (p. 56)
tawny (p. 66)
hoopskirt (p. 68)
ox goad (p. 68)
molasses (p. 69)
jumper pocket (p. 78)
contradicting (p. 79)
flutterbudget (p. 95)
plank (p. 102)

yoked (p. 52)
stubble land (p. 53)
straw-stack (p. 53)
bole (p. 65)
grasshopper weather (p. 66)
challis (p. 68)
corn dodgers (p. 69)
pshaw (p. 77)
hoarhound candy (p. 78)
shawls (p. 94)
Jiminy crickets (p. 97)
current (p. 102)

Questions:

1. Why do you think the girls are disobedient about the straw-stack when they are so obedient at other times?

2. What do you think "grasshopper weather" means?

3. Why does the family go to so much trouble to get ready to go to town?

4. Why does Laura say, "I think I like wolves better than cattle"? (p. 79)

5. Why do you think the girls are willing to give up their Christmas presents for the horses?

6. Who is the button-string really for, Carrie or Laura and Mary? Explain.

7. When Laura goes into the creek she thinks, "This is not like wolves or cattle." What does she mean by that? (p. 104)

58 / On the Banks of Plum Creek

8. How is Laura changed by going into the roaring creek?

9. Why are the girls usually obedient and always truthful?

Chapters 16-20:

boughten (p. 111)
partition (p. 111)
hinges (p. 114)
oblong (p. 115)
shepherdess (p. 122)
bloodsuckers (p. 132)
buffalo fish (p. 139)
catfish (p. 139)
bullheads (p. 139)
meadow larks (p. 142)
prairie hens (p. 142)
fidget (p. 151)

shingles (p. 111)
lean-to (p. 112)
draught (p. 115)
bracket (p. 122)
leeches (p. 132)
cipher (p. 138)
pickerel (p. 139)
shiners (p. 139)
blue heron (p. 142)
snipes (p. 142)
slate (p. 151)

Questions:

1. Sketch out a floor plan of the new house.

2. What are the advantages and disadvantages of the new house that Pa built over the dugout?

3. Read the conversations between Ma and Pa on pages 109 and 119-120. How are their viewpoints different? Why do you think this is so?

4. Why doesn't Laura want to go to school?

5. Why do you think Nellie Oleson has such scorn for country girls?

6. How does Laura feel about school? How does Mary feel about school?

Chapters 21-26:

Vocabulary:

beholden (p. 153)
velocipede (p. 162)
hospitality (p. 168)
home missionary (p. 178)
belfry (p. 182)
pitch the hymn (p. 188)
manure-pile (p. 197)

posies (p. 160)
jumping-jack (p. 163)
vanity cakes (p. 169)
crocheted (p. 179)
cravat (p. 183)
tuning-fork (p. 188)
tobacco-juice (p. 205)

Questions:

1. Why do you think Nellie Oleson made a point of inviting Laura and Christy to her party?

2. What remarkable things did Laura see at Nellie's house? What made these things so remarkable to her?

3. Which party do you think the girls liked best, the town party or the country party? Why?

4. Why does Laura suddenly decide she likes Sunday school? (p. 187)

5. Why do you think Pa decided to spend $3 on a church bell instead of boots for himself?

6. Whose life is most changed by the grasshoppers? Explain.

Chapters 27-32:

Vocabulary:

dust devils (p. 213)
plague of locusts (p. 216)
patchwork (p. 236)
bolts (of cloth) (p. 241)
shouldercape (p. 242)
muskrat (p. 245)
mink (p. 245)
drawers (underwear) (p. 248)
lavish (p. 251)
churn (p. 252)
mosquito-bar bag (p. 253)
threadbare (p. 257)
bobsled (p. 259)
ancestral home (p. 267)

moquito-netting (p. 215)
knoll (p. 223)
comforters (p. 236)
flannel (p. 242)
kerosene-can (p. 243)
otter (p. 245)
scholars (p. 246)
petticoats (p. 248)
washboard (p. 252)
dasher (p. 252)
woolly muffler (p. 253)
fastenings (p. 257)
chinook (p. 259)

Questions:

1. "All day long Laura missed Pa, and at night when the wind blew lonesomely over the dark land, she felt hollow and aching." (p. 224) Why does Laura miss Pa so much?

2. Why does Ma cry when they get the letter from Pa, when she hadn't cried before this? (p. 226)

3. Why do you think Ma insists that Laura give Charlotte to Anna?

4. Why is Laura so upset when she finds Charlotte in a puddle of water?

5. Reread page 267. Why do you think the grasshoppers all went west at the same time?

60 / On the Banks of Plum Creek

Chapters 33-41:

Vocabulary

gunnysack (p. 274)
blizzards (p. 281)
scudding (p. 295)
buffalo overcoat (p. 300)
bean-porridge hot (p. 309)
cat's cradle (p. 322)

prairie fire (p. 276)
beaver meadow (p. 283)
frost-bitten (p. 300)
earlaps (p. 301)
Pussy-in-the-corner (p. 316)
oyster crackers (p. 330)

Questions:

1. Why are Ma and the girls less concerned about Pa's leaving to find work the second time?

2. Why do you think Pa suggests that he and Ma go into town for no particular reason? (p. 283)

3. Why does Pa go into town for tobacco and news even though it's bitterly cold and he is not dressed for it? (p. 299)

4. How do the pictures Laura draws in the frost reflect what she is thinking? Why do you think she drew those things?

5. Why doesn't Ma put a lamp in the window the second night of the blizzard?

6. Why did Pa keep walking in the storm instead of sitting down to rest?

7. Of the three Christmases described in the story, which one do you think is the happiest for the Ingalls family? Why?

8. The Ingalls face many hardships in this story. In spite of this, the overall feeling of the book is happy. Why?

9. Look at the book's illustrations. How does the artwork reflect the text? Why do you think the artist chose to illustrate those particular events in the story? Which events would you have have chosen to illustrate?

RELATED BOOKS

Other books in the Little House series:
Little House in the Big Woods, 1953.
Farmer Boy, 1953.
Little House on the Prairie, 1953.
By the Shores of Silver Lake, 1953.
The Long Winter, 1953.
Little Town on the Prairie, 1953.
These Happy Golden Years, 1953.

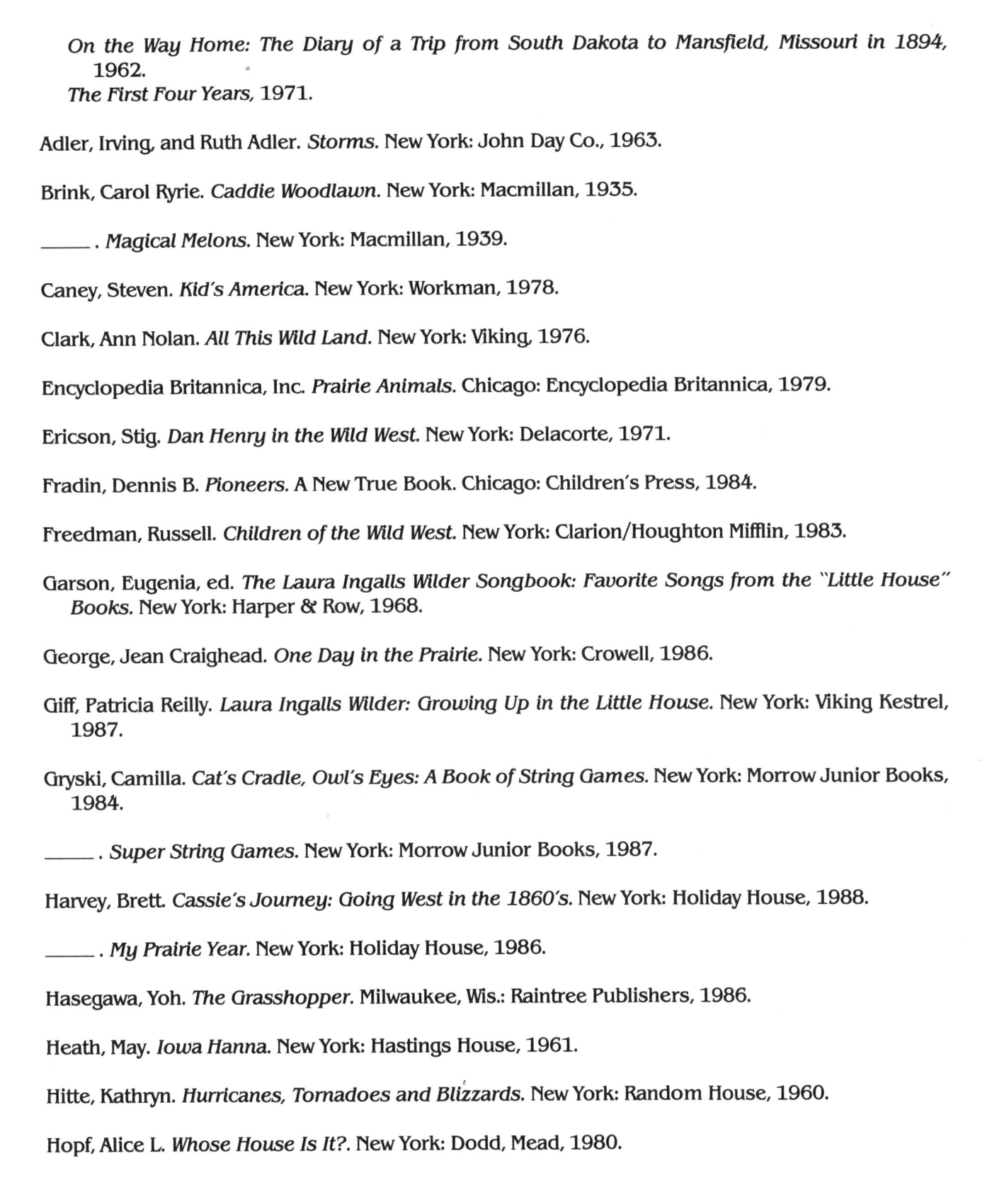

On the Way Home: The Diary of a Trip from South Dakota to Mansfield, Missouri in 1894, 1962.

The First Four Years, 1971.

Adler, Irving, and Ruth Adler. *Storms.* New York: John Day Co., 1963.

Brink, Carol Ryrie. *Caddie Woodlawn.* New York: Macmillan, 1935.

———. *Magical Melons.* New York: Macmillan, 1939.

Caney, Steven. *Kid's America.* New York: Workman, 1978.

Clark, Ann Nolan. *All This Wild Land.* New York: Viking, 1976.

Encyclopedia Britannica, Inc. *Prairie Animals.* Chicago: Encyclopedia Britannica, 1979.

Ericson, Stig. *Dan Henry in the Wild West.* New York: Delacorte, 1971.

Fradin, Dennis B. *Pioneers.* A New True Book. Chicago: Children's Press, 1984.

Freedman, Russell. *Children of the Wild West.* New York: Clarion/Houghton Mifflin, 1983.

Garson, Eugenia, ed. *The Laura Ingalls Wilder Songbook: Favorite Songs from the "Little House" Books.* New York: Harper & Row, 1968.

George, Jean Craighead. *One Day in the Prairie.* New York: Crowell, 1986.

Giff, Patricia Reilly. *Laura Ingalls Wilder: Growing Up in the Little House.* New York: Viking Kestrel, 1987.

Gryski, Camilla. *Cat's Cradle, Owl's Eyes: A Book of String Games.* New York: Morrow Junior Books, 1984.

———. *Super String Games.* New York: Morrow Junior Books, 1987.

Harvey, Brett. *Cassie's Journey: Going West in the 1860's.* New York: Holiday House, 1988.

———. *My Prairie Year.* New York: Holiday House, 1986.

Hasegawa, Yoh. *The Grasshopper.* Milwaukee, Wis.: Raintree Publishers, 1986.

Heath, May. *Iowa Hanna.* New York: Hastings House, 1961.

Hitte, Kathryn. *Hurricanes, Tornadoes and Blizzards.* New York: Random House, 1960.

Hopf, Alice L. *Whose House Is It?.* New York: Dodd, Mead, 1980.

Horn, Madeline Darrough. *The New Home.* New York: Scribner's, 1962.

Hutchins, Ross E. *Grasshoppers and Their Kin.* New York: Dodd, Mead, 1972.

Kalman, Bobbie. *Early Christmas.* New York: Crabtree Publishing Co., 1981.

_____. *Early Family Home.* New York: Crabtree Publishing Co., 1982.

_____. *Early Schools.* New York: Crabtree Publishing Co., 1982.

_____. *Early Settler Children.* New York: Crabtree Publishing Co., 1982.

Lerner, Carol. *Seasons of the Tallgrass Prairie.* New York: Morrow, 1980.

MacBride, Roger Lea, ed. *West from Home: Letters of Laura Ingalls Wilder to Almanzo Wilder, San Francisco, 1915.* New York: Harper & Row, 1974.

MacLachlan, Patricia. *Sarah, Plain and Tall.* New York: Harper & Row, 1985.

May, Charles Paul. *Strangers in the Storm.* New York: Abelard-Schuman, 1972.

Porter, Keith. *Discovering Crickets and Grasshoppers.* New York: Bookwright Press, 1986.

Ross, Frank. *Storms and Man.* New York: Lothrop, Lee & Shepard, 1971.

Rowan, James P. *Prairies and Grasslands.* Chicago: Children's Press, 1983.

Sloane, Eric. *Once upon a Time.* New York: Hastings House, 1982.

Talbot, Charlene Joy. *An Orphan for Nebraska.* New York: Atheneum, 1979.

Time-Life Books, ed. *The Pioneers.* New York: Time-Life Books, 1974.

Tunis, Edwin. *Frontier Living.* New York: World Publishing Co., 1961.

Walker, Barbara Muhs. *The Little House Cookbook: Frontier Foods from Laura Ingalls Wilder's Classic Stories.* New York: Harper & Row, 1979.

Zochert, Donald. *Laura: The Life of Laura Ingalls Wilder.* New York: Regnery, 1976.

ENRICHMENT ACTIVITIES

On the Banks of Plum Creek

1. Learn a song from *The Laura Ingalls Wilder Songbook* and perform it for the group.

2. Prepare one (or more) of the recipes from *The Little House Cookbook*.

3. Build a model of a dugout.

4. Make a map of the Ingalls farm and the surrounding area.

5. Make a poster or mural showing the plants and animals mentioned in the book. Label your illustrations.

6. Make a stuffed doll like Charlotte.

7. Find out more about one-room schoolhouses like the one Laura and Mary attended. How is the room arranged? What did the furniture look like? What books and materials did they use? Draw a picture to help you share the information with the group.

8. Find out more about grasshoppers and locusts. What causes a grasshopper infestation like the one described in the story?

9. Find out about games and toys from the 1800s. Draw pictures of them to help you share the information with the group.

10. Learn how to play a couple of string games like cat's cradle. Demonstrate them for the group.

11. Write a report telling about blizzards. What is a blizzard? What causes them? Where and when are they most likely to occur? Locate pictures of blizzards to help you share your information with the group.

12. Write an account of Laura's party as Nellie might have written it in her diary. Be sure to tell the story from Nellie's point of view.

13. If Charlotte could talk, what would she have told Laura about her adventures after Anna Nelson took her home? Write Charlotte's story.

14. Read one of the other books in the Little House series by Laura Ingalls Wilder.

15. Create your own activity for *On the Banks of Plum Creek*.

16. These are some of the sayings that Ma and Pa used to teach their values to Laura and Mary. Choose one of these sayings, write it at the top of a piece of paper, tell what you think it means, and give an example of a situation in which this saying would be true.

    "What must be done is best done cheerfully." (p. 8)

    "All's well that ends well." (p. 8)

    "If you don't want trouble, don't go looking for it." (p. 133)

    "We must not accept hospitality without making some return." (p. 168)

    "It'll never be noticed on a trotting horse." (p. 180)

    "There's no great loss without some gain." (p. 199)

    "We'll pull through somehow." (p. 203)

    "The darkest hour is just before dawn." (p. 228)

    "The time will go faster if we think of other things." (p. 228)

    "There is nothing in the world so good as good neighbors." (p. 275)

Sidewalk Story

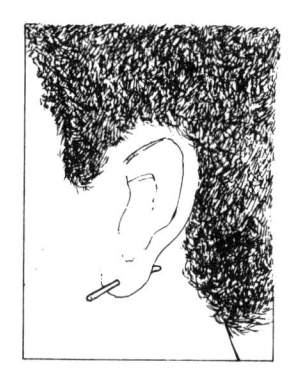

Author: Sharon Bell Mathis

Publisher, Date: Viking, 1971

Pages: 58

SUMMARY

This is a story of friendship and determination set in the inner city. Lilly Etta's best friend, Tanya, and her family are being evicted from their home, and no adult has the courage to help them. Lilly Etta draws attention to the situation in an unusual manner, and she succeeds in a surprising way.

PRE-READING/MOTIVATIONAL ACTIVITIES

1. Ask the students to read the title and look at the picture on the cover of the book. Ask them these questions.
   What do you think the story is going to be about?
   Who do you think the main character is going to be?
   What do you think is the setting of the story?

2. Bring in human-interest newspaper articles. Have students bring in human-interest stories from the local paper.

3. Tape and show a human-interest story from a television news program. Discuss why this kind of story would be shown on a news program.

4. Talk about friendship. Ask students how much have they been or would they be willing to sacrifice for a friend?

5. Talk about the homeless. Ask students: Who are the homeless? How do people become homeless? If possible, use articles from the local newspaper to promote discussion.

VOCABULARY/DISCUSSION QUESTIONS

Vocabulary:

straws in ears (p. 1)
greens (p. 5)
"put Ruth out" (p. 7)
banister (p. 19)

stoop (p. 1)
(Social Security) checks (p. 7)
marshal (p. 16)
tarpaulin (p. 50)

66 / Sidewalk Story

Questions:

1. Why do people stand around and watch people in trouble without doing or saying anything?

2. Why do you think Lilly Etta's mother doesn't want to say good-by to Mrs. Brown?

3. Why didn't Mrs. Brown or Tanya ask for help from their friends?

4. Why do you think Lilly Etta is willing to risk so much to help her friend?

5. Why did Lilly Etta tell the reporter that she was 50 years old? (p. 32)

6. It says on page 51, "She didn't dare look at her mother." Why not?

7. How did Mrs. Allen feel about Lilly Etta's efforts to help the Browns?

8. What part did the earrings play in the story?

9. When Lilly Etta calls the reporter he tells her, ". . . it's not a real news story. It happens all the time. . . . The only thing unusual in all this is you." What is so unusual about Lilly Etta?

10. Why do you think the reporter changed his mind about covering the story?

RELATED BOOKS

Carlsen, Natalie Savage. *Marchers for the Dream.* New York: Harper & Row, 1969.

Feelings, Tom. *Daydreamers.* New York: Dial, 1981.

———. *Something on My Mind.* New York: Dial, 1978.

Flournoy, Valerie. *The Patchwork Quilt.* New York: Dial, 1985.

Greenfield, Eloise. *Talk about a Family.* Philadelphia: Lippincott, 1978.

Jordan, June. *Kimako's Story.* Boston: Houghton Mifflin, 1981.

Lexau, Joan. *Striped Ice Cream.* New York: Lippincott, 1968.

Mathis, Sharon Bell. *The Hundred Penny Box.* New York: Viking, 1975.

Yarbrough, Camille. *Cornrows.* New York: Coward, McCann & Geoghegan, 1979.

ENRICHMENT ACTIVITIES

Sidewalk Story

1. Discuss things that ordinary citizens can do to help the homeless. Call local agencies to see what is being done in your community. Present this information to the group.

2. Plan a project to help a local agency that serves people who do not have adequate food, clothing, or shelter.

3. Do a writing activity about friendship, for example, "What Is a Friend?"

4. Lilly Etta succeeds because she is able to persuade others to help her friends. Write a letter of persuasion to a newspaper, a magazine, an agency, or an institution on a subject of your choice.

5. When Mrs. Brown could no longer pay her rent the marshals came to move her out of her home. Find out what happens to someone in your community who can no longer pay their rent. Report your findings to the group.

6. Survey the students in your class. How many have pierced ears? How old were they when their ears were pierced? Graph the results of your survey.

7. Interview people of all ages who have pierced ears about their ear-piercing experiences. Write a paragraph about two or three of the most interesting experiences.

8. Find human-interest stories in the newspaper. Share them with the group.

9. The paperback edition of *Sidewalk Story* does not have any illustrations. Select two or three scenes from the story and make illustrations for them.

10. Create your own activity for *Sidewalk Story*.

Stone Fox

Author: John Reynolds Gardiner

Illustrator: Marcia Sewall

Publisher, Date: Harper & Row, 1980

Pages: 81

SUMMARY

Little Willy is desperately seeking a way to earn the money needed to save his grandfather's farm. Willy and his dog, Searchlight, run the dogsled race of their lives against Stone Fox, a powerful man who has never lost a race.

PRE-READING/MOTIVATIONAL ACTIVITIES

1. Ask the students to read the title and look at the picture on the cover of the book. Ask them these questions:
    What do you think the story is going to be about?
    Who do you think the main characters are going to be?
    Who or what is Stone Fox?

2. Locate Jackson, Wyoming on a map. Look at photographs and/or filmstrips showing the Rocky Mountain region of the country to give students a clearer picture of the setting of the story.

VOCABULARY/DISCUSSION QUESTIONS

Chapters 1-5:

Vocabulary:

chicken coop (p. 4)	searchlight (p. 5)
harmonica (p. 7)	palomino (p. 7)
medically (p. 10)	irrigation (p. 12)
strongbox (p. 17)	on credit (p. 17)
city slickers (p. 26)	forged (p. 28)
twang of a ricocheting bullet (p. 30)	authority (p. 32)
general store (p. 42)	Samoyeds (p. 45)

Questions:

1. Why do you think Grandfather is sick? Why has he given up?

2. What kind of person is Willy? How did he become that kind of person?

3. Prediction: What do you think Willy will do about the taxes?

Chapters 6-8:

Vocabulary:

hair tonic (p. 46)
cunning (p. 51)
treacherous (p. 57)

amateurs (p. 47)
Arapaho (p. 53)

Questions:

1. Do you think it is wise or foolish for Willy to spend all his money on the entry fee? Explain your answer.

2. What do we find out about Stone Fox? If he were willing to talk to the people of the town, what do you think he would say?

3. At the beginning of the race, why do Stone Fox's eyes "lack the sparkle little Willie remembered seeing before"?

4. Prediction: Write a description of what you think will happen in the race.

Chapters 9-10:

Vocabulary:

disqualified (p. 71)
challenger (p. 78)

Questions:

1. Why did Willy risk everything for the farm?

2. Why do you think Stone Fox helped Willy win the race?

3. Who needed to win the race more, Stone Fox or Willy?

4. On the surface, Willy and Stone Fox seem quite different. In what ways are they alike?

5. Why didn't Willy get mad at his grandfather? At the tax collector? At Stone Fox?

6. Does the author give any hint that Searchlight will die?

7. Do you think Willy would have run the race if he had known what was going to happen to Searchlight?

8. Why is Searchlight a good name for the dog? Why is Stone Fox a good name for the Indian?

9. Is Stone Fox portrayed as more than human or less than human? How does this fit in with common stereotypes of Indians.

10. Why didn't the author tell us what happened after the race?

11. What do *you* think happens next?

12. Do you think this is a true story or a legend? Explain.

13. Look at the book's illustrations. How does the artwork reflect the text? Why do you think the artist chose to illustrate those particular events in the story? Which events would you have chosen to illustrate?

RELATED BOOKS

Gardiner, John Reynolds. *Top Secret*. Boston: Little, Brown, 1984.

Heady, Eleanor. *Sage Smoke; Tales of the Shoshoni-Bannock Indians*. Chicago: Follett, 1973.

Levenson, Dorothy. *Homesteaders and Indians*. New York: Watts, 1971.

O'Dell, Scott. *Black Star, Bright Dawn*. Boston: Houghton Mifflin, 1988.

Powers, William K. *Indians of the Northern Plains*. New York: Putnam, 1969.

Reit, Seymour. *Race against Death: A True Story of the Far North*. New York: Dodd, Mead, 1976.

Sheppard, Sally. *Indians of the Plains*. New York: Watts, 1976.

Smith, Doris Buchanan. *Salted Lemons*. New York: Four Winds, 1980.

RELATED MAGAZINE ARTICLES

Jacqueline Geschickter. "Go, Team, Go." *National Geographic World* 172 (December, 1989): 3-7.

Kathryn Kelley. "A Race to Spark Learning." *Learning 89* 17, 6 (February 1989): 40-44.

ENRICHMENT ACTIVITIES

Stone Fox

1. Find out more about dogsled racing. What breeds of dogs are used? How fast and how far do they go? Are dogsleds still used for everyday transportation? Share your findings with the class. If possible, show the group some pictures.

2. Make a diorama of the race.

3. Make a model of a dogsled.

4. Make a map of the race course. Be sure to include all of the landmarks mentioned in the story.

5. Learn more about Stone Fox and his cause. Locate information about the history of the Shoshone and Arapaho Indians in Wyoming.

6. Write a letter: If Stone Fox had written Willy a letter explaining why he wanted to win the race, what would he have written?

7. Write name poems that describe Searchlight, Stone Fox, and Willy:

```
S              S              W
E              T              I
A              O              L
R              N              L
C              E              Y
H              F
L              O
I              X
G
H
T
```

8. Create your own activity for *Stone Fox*.

A Taste of Blackberries

Author: Doris Buchanan Smith

Illustrator: Charles Robinson

Publisher, Date: Crowell/Scholastic, 1973

Pages: 73

SUMMARY

This is a novel told in the first person by a young boy whose best friend, Jamie, was always taking foolish risks. When Jamie was stung by the bees he provoked, no one was surprised. His friends were concerned when the ambulance came to take Jamie away and shocked when they heard he had died. This story tells how a young boy deals with his best friend's death.

PRE-READING/MOTIVATIONAL ACTIVITIES

1. Ask the students to read the title and look at the picture on the cover of the book. Ask these questions:
   What do you think the story is going to be about?
   Who do you think the main characters are going to be?
   What do you think is the setting of the story?

2. Ask students to write a short paragraph describing a good friend, making sure to include things they like and dislike about that person. When they are through writing, ask them how it is possible to be a friend to someone who sometimes does or says things you don't like. What do they do when this happens?

3. Read the first two pages of the book aloud to the group. Explain to the students that this book is written in the first person and that all of the events in the story are seen from only one person's point of view.

VOCABULARY/DISCUSSION QUESTIONS

Chapters 1-3:

Vocabulary:

    thicket (p. 1)
    brambles (p. 2)
    aggravate (p. 2)
    scornfully (p. 5)
    paradiddles (p. 7)
    buoy (p. 8)
    chauffeur (p. 16)
    kidnapper (p. 18)
    rummaged (p. 24)
    dirt daubs (p. 29)

    blackberry patch (p. 1)
    exaggeration (p. 2)
    tiresome (p. 3)
    boundary line (p. 5)
    false confidence (p. 7)
    Japanese beetles (p. 10)
    tongue-tied (p. 17)
    uncanniest (p. 19)
    bird sanctuary (p. 25)

Questions:

1. What kind of boy is Jamie? Give some examples to support your opinion.

2. What kind of boy is the narrator? Give some examples to support your opinion.

3. Why do you think these two boys are friends?

4. Why do you think the narrator has a hard time saying no to Jamie?

5. Do you think Jamie is daring or foolish?

6. The narrator gets angry at Jamie when he flops on the ground after getting stung. Why does this make him so much angrier than Jamie's other pranks?

7. Prediction: What do you think is going to happen to Jamie?

Chapters 4-8:

Vocabulary:

    unconsciousness (p. 32)
    miracle (p. 33)
    writhing (p. 34)
    freak accident (p. 36)
    communications system (p. 37)

    conscience (p. 32)
    instinct (p. 33)
    allergic (p. 34)
    rose trellis (p. 37)
    Morse code (p. 39)

(vocabulary continues on next page)

74 / A Taste of Blackberries

funeral parlor (p. 40)
britches (p. 52)
casket (p. 62)
droning (p. 62)
taboo (p. 63)

radiant (p. 51)
counselor (p. 55)
chrysanthemums (p. 62)
procession (p. 63)

Questions:

1. How do Jamie's antics contribute to his own death?

2. What is a freak accident?

3. How do the narrator's thoughts about Jamie change when he finds out Jamie has died?

4. The narrator deals with Jamie's death in different ways as the story progresses. List the ways in the order they occur.

5. On page 54 Mrs. Mullins says, "Honey, one of the hardest things we have to learn is that some questions do not have answers." What does she mean? Why is the narrator grateful that she gave him an honest answer?

6. How does Jamie's death change the narrator?

7. How do the adults try to help the narrator in different ways?

8. Why do you think the author called this book *A Taste of Blackberries*?

9. Why do you think the author chose to tell this story in the first person?

10. Look at the book's illustrations. How does the artwork reflect the text? Why do you think the artist chose to illustrate those particular events in the story? Which events would you have chosen to illustrate?

Leader:

Read *The Saddest Time,* by Norma Simon, to the group. Ask which of the three stories in the book is the most like *A Taste of Blackberries*. Discuss all three stories in relation to *A Taste of Blackberries.*

RELATED BOOKS

Bauer, Marion Dane. *On My Honor.* New York: Houghton Mifflin/Dell, 1986.

Clifton, Lucille. *Everett Anderson's Goodbye.* New York: Henry Holt and Company, 1983.

Cohn, Janice. *I Had a Friend Named Peter.* New York: Morrow, 1987.

Fassler, Joan. *My Grandpa Died Today.* New York: Human Science Press, 1983.

Greene, Constance. *Beat the Turtle Drum.* New York: Viking, 1976.

Lee, Virginia. *The Magic Moth.* New York: Seabury, 1972.

Lowry, Lois. *A Summer to Die.* New York: Houghton Mifflin, 1977.

Paterson, Katherine. *Bridge to Terabithia.* New York: Crowell, 1977.

Richter, Elizabeth. *Losing Someone You Love: When a Brother or Sister Dies.* New York: Putnam, 1986.

Silverstein, Alvin. *Allergies.* Philadelphia: Lippincott, 1977.

Silverstein, Alvin, and Virginia Silverstein. *Itch, Sniffle and Sneeze.* New York: Four Winds, 1978.

Simon, Norma. *The Saddest Time.* Chicago: Whitman, 1986.

_____. *We Remember Philip.* Chicago: Whitman, 1979.

Smith, Doris Buchanan. *Kelly's Creek.* New York: Crowell, 1975.

_____. *Last Was Lloyd.* New York: Viking, 1981.

_____. *Salted Lemons.* New York: Four Winds, 1980.

Wilder, Laura Ingalls. *Little House in the Big Woods.* New York: Harper & Row, 1953.

ENRICHMENT ACTIVITIES
A Taste of Blackberries

1. Find out if someone in your school is allergic to bee stings. Interview that person to find out the effect of a bee sting and what to do to counteract this effect. Report your findings to the group.

2. Do research on bee stings.
    - Why do bees sting?
    - How do bees sting?
    - What happens to the bee after it stings?
    - Why does it hurt the person who is stung?
    - What is the first-aid treatment for bee stings?

    Report your findings to the group.

3. Make a first-aid poster showing how to treat bee stings.

4. Read *My Grandpa Died Today* by Joan Fassler. Compare the experiences of the narrators of this story and of *A Taste of Blackberries*. To tell how their experiences are alike and different, complete a chart like the one below:

	My Grandpa Died Today	*A Taste of Blackberries*
How are the stories alike?		
How are the stories different?		

5. Read chapter 11, "The Harvest," in *Little House in the Big Woods* by Laura Ingalls Wilder. Compare Charley and Jamie:
    - What kind of kids are they?
    - Why are they stung by bees?
    - What are the consequences of their actions?

    Tell the group about Cousin Charley, and explain how he and Jamie are alike.

6. Write a letter that the narrator might have written to Jamie's mother, telling her the things he couldn't say to her after Jamie's death.

7. Should children be allowed to attend funerals? What do *you* think? Write an opinion paper giving reasons that support your answer.

8. Read another book by Doris Buchanan Smith (*see* Related Books).

9. Create your own activity for *A Taste of Blackberries*.

GRADE FOUR

Follow My Leader

Author: James B. Garfield

Illustrator: Don Sibley

Publisher, Date: Viking, 1957

Pages: 187

SUMMARY

Eleven-year-old Jimmy is blinded by a carelessly thrown firecracker. With the help of friends, family, and a social worker he learns the skills necessary to cope with his disability. When Jimmy finally gets his own guide dog, Leader, he is able to return to school and Boy Scouts with renewed confidence in his abilities.

PRE-READING/MOTIVATIONAL ACTIVITIES

1. Ask the students to read the title and look at the picture on the cover of the book. Ask them these questions:
    What do you think the story is going to be about?
    Who do you think the main characters are going to be?
    What do you think is the setting of the story?

2. Read a short book or article on blindness that gives children some background information about the causes of blindness and how blind people compensate for their visual impairment (*see* Related Books).

VOCABULARY/DISCUSSION QUESTIONS

Chapters 1-4:

Vocabulary:

gesture (p. 1)
rookie (p. 2)
sizzler (p. 3)

authority (p. 2)
deliberately (p. 2)
down the groove (p. 3)

(vocabulary continues on next page)

78 / Follow My Leader

hand grenade (p. 4)
critical condition (p. 8)
nectar (p. 9)
unblemished (p. 9)
disfigured (p. 12)
handicapped (p. 12)
guide dog (p. 15)
defiant (p. 18)
4-H Clubs (p. 21)
Braille (p. 23)
short-wave station (p. 23)
fighter bomber (p. 25)
turret gunner (p. 25)
facial vision (p. 29)
spruced up (p. 38)
telegraphy (p. 39)
Louis Braille (p. 41)
universal (p. 42)
unaccustomed (p. 42)

demolition squad (p. 5)
mummified (p. 9)
Greek gods (p. 9)
gauze (p. 11)
welfare worker (p. 12)
orderly (hospital) (p. 13)
self-confidence (p. 17)
seared (p. 18)
noncommittal (p. 21)
amateur (p. 23)
antenna (p. 24)
navigator (p. 25)
Sherlock Holmes (p. 26)
third eye (p. 29)
Morse code (p. 39)
primer (p. 39)
awl (p. 41)
international (p. 42)

Questions:

1. Why do you think Mike lit the firecracker when all the others agreed that it was unsafe?

2. What do you think Jimmy was like before the accident?

3. What does Jimmy's dream mean? (pp. 15-16)

4. Why does Mrs. Carter want Jimmy to wear dark glasses?

5. What do you think Mike was like before the accident?

6. Why do you think Jimmy is so negative about the guide dog? (p. 15)

7. What is Jimmy's mother like? Do you think she will be of any help to him?

8. What is Carolyn like? Do you think she will be of any help to Jimmy?

9. Prediction: What does Miss Thompson mean when she says, "I told you there are many other ways of seeing and you will learn to use them"? (p. 45)

Follow My Leader / 79

Chapters 5-9:

Vocabulary:

radar set (p. 47)
nocturnal (p. 48)
technicians (p. 51)
merit badges (p. 54)
landmarks (p. 57)
characters (letters) (p. 61)
stylus (p. 78)
Niagara Falls (p. 91)

electronics (p. 47)
compressed (p. 50)
conspiracies (p. 53)
travelogue lecture (p. 55)
abbreviations (p. 61)
tormentor (p. 72)
redcap (p. 82)
megaphone (p. 92)

Questions:

1. What things did Miss Thompson teach Jimmy and in what order did she teach them? Do you think there is a logical order to the skills she is teaching him?

2. Why does Jimmy choose this time to give his bat and glove to Chuck and Art? (pp. 66-67)

3. Reread page 77. Why do you think the women in the store assumed Jimmy couldn't hear them?

4. Why are the people on the bus so anxious to do things for Jimmy? (pp. 84-86)

5. Prediction: What things, besides how to use his guide dog, will Jimmy learn at the school?

Chapters 10-13:

Vocabulary:

Sirius (p. 99)
German shepherd (p. 100)
currycomb (p. 100)
Orion (p. 102)
constellation (p. 102)
light-year (p. 102)
muzzle (p. 110)
diplomas (p. 121)
hostess (p. 123)
dachshund (p. 132)

pedigreed (p. 100)
groom (p. 100)
mythology (p. 102)
Artemis (p. 102)
southern hemisphere (p. 102)
bull terrier (p. 110)
tiddly-wink (p. 112)
reception (p. 121)
administration building (p. 128)

Questions:

1. Do you think the rules at the school are too strict? Why or why not?

2. Why doesn't Jimmy want to call his dog Sirius?

80 / Follow My Leader

3. In what ways does Leader give Jimmy confidence?

4. What would you do and how would you feel if you were in Mike's position? (pp. 119-120)

5. How are the things Jimmy learned at the guide dog school different from the things he learned from Miss Thompson?

6. In what ways did Jimmy's teachers teach him how to "fit in" as a blind person in society? What advice did they have for him? How does a blind person go about "fitting in" to a sighted world? (pp. 51, 111-112, 116)

7. Prediction: How will Jimmy's life change now that he has Leader?

Chapters 14-17:

Vocabulary:

superintendent (p. 142)
Juvenile Hall (p. 152)
emphatic (p. 166)
swanky (p. 185)

State School for the Blind (p. 142)
quarantined (p. 165)
straitjacket (p. 173)
honorary (p. 186)

Questions:

1. Is the superintendent being fair when he tells Jimmy that Leader can't come to school? (p. 142)

2. Why do you think Jimmy wants Leader at school with him?

3. Besides Leader, which of the characters in the story was most helpful to Jimmy? Explain.

4. Look at the book's illustrations. How does the artwork reflect the text? Why do you think the artist chose to illustrate those particular events in the story? Which events would you have chosen to illustrate?

RELATED BOOKS

Boy Scouts of America. *Boy Scouts Fieldbook*. New York: Workman Publishing Co., 1978.

Butler, Beverly Kathleen. *Light a Single Candle*. New York: Dodd, Mead, 1962.

Curtis, Patricia. *Cindy: A Hearing Ear Dog*. New York: E. P. Dutton, 1981.

_____. *Greff: The Story of a Guide Dog*. New York: E. P. Dutton, 1982.

Hillcourt, William. *Official Boy Scout Handbook*. 9th ed. New Brunswick, N.J.: Boy Scouts of America, 1979.

Hunter, Edith Fisher. *Child of the Silent Night.* Boston: Houghton Mifflin, 1963.

Keeler, Stephen. *Louis Braille.* New York: Bookwright Press, 1986.

Marcus, Rebecca B. *Being Blind.* New York: Hastings House, 1981.

Putnam, Peter. *The Triumph of the Seeing Eye.* New York: Harper & Row, 1963.

Rappaport, Eva. *"Banner Forward!" The Pictorial Biography of a Guide Dog.* New York: E. P. Dutton, 1969.

Sullivan, Mary Beth, Alan J. Brightman, and Joseph Blatt. *Feeling Free.* New York: Addison-Wesley, 1979.

Weiss, Malcolm. *Seeing through the Dark: Blind and Sighted—A Vision Shared.* New York: Harcourt Brace Jovanovich, 1976.

Wepman, Dennis. *Helen Keller.* New York: Chelsea House, 1987.

Wilder, Laura Ingalls. *By the Shores of Silver Lake.* New York: Harper & Row, 1953.

Wolf, Bernard. *Connie's New Eyes.* New York: Lippincott, 1976.

Popular children's books written in Braille are available from:
   Children's Braille Book Club
   National Braille Press Inc.
   88 Saint Stephen St.
   Boston, MA 02115
   (617) 266-6160

82 / Follow My Leader

ENRICHMENT ACTIVITIES

Follow My Leader

1. Do a report on the life of Louis Braille.

2. What causes blindness? Make a list of the various causes of blindness and share what you have learned with the group.

3. Make a diagram or a model of the human eye. Using your model, explain how our eyes work.

4. What are the laws in your state regulating the sale and use of fireworks? Should the laws be more strict than they are? Write a short essay explaining your opinion.

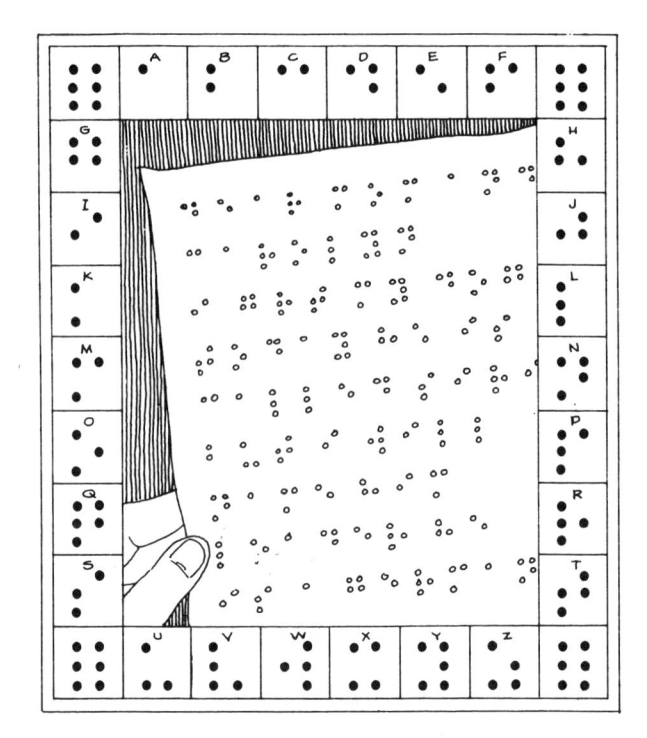

5. Read about leader dogs for the blind. Give an oral report to the group. Be sure to include the history of the program, how leader dogs are raised and trained, and rules and regulations affecting them.

6. Arrange for someone with a guide dog to visit your class. Before the speaker arrives, write a list of questions you want to ask.

7. Create and do an experiment that demonstrates how we get information from our other senses when we are unable to see. (For example, can students distinguish salt, sugar, oatmeal, rice, and flour by the sounds they make when shaken in a closed container?)

8. What is your most valuable sense: sight, hearing, smell, touch, or taste? Write a paragraph explaining why this sense is most valuable to you.

9. Invite a Boy Scout leader to your class to talk about scouting. Before the speaker arrives, write a list of questions you want to ask.

10. Read about the care and training of guide dogs. Draw or compile a series of pictures that will help you explain what you learn. Be sure to include a diagram of the dog's special harness.

11. Decode the Braille message on this page. Continue Jimmy's letter using the Braille alphabet.

12. Mack asks Jimmy, "How would you like to go through life knowing you made someone else go blind?" (chapter 12) Write the events in the story from Mike's point of view.

13. Create your own activity for *Follow My Leader*.

Homer Price

Author: Robert McCloskey

Illustrator: Robert McCloskey

Publisher, Date: Viking/Scholastic, 1943

Pages: 160

SUMMARY

Homer Price is the main character of these six humorous short stories, which take place in the small midwestern town of Centerburg. This collection includes "The Doughnuts," a sorcerer's apprentice-like tale of an out-of-control doughnut machine and a missing diamond bracelet.

GENERAL PRE-READING/MOTIVATIONAL ACTIVITIES

1. Discuss the copyright date (1943). How was everyday life different in the 1930s and 1940s from the way it is now?

2. Discuss the main character. Ask the group to read pages 8-11 and look at the picture of Homer on page 11. What do we learn about Homer in these first few pages?

3. Tell the group that this book is made up of six short stories about Homer Price and the people of Centerburg. Each story may be read without reading the others, but they are more enjoyable when read together.

PRE-READING/MOTIVATIONAL ACTIVITIES/VOCABULARY/DISCUSSION QUESTIONS

"The Case of the Sensational Scent"

Vocabulary:

scent (p. 7)
tourist (p. 8)
icebox (p. 9)

sensational (p. 7)
aroma (p. 9)
slogan (p. 12)

84 / Homer Price

Questions:

1. Normally robbers with guns would be very frightening. How did the author make these robbers funny rather than frightening? Why do you think he did that?

2. How was Aroma helpful in the capture of the robbers?

3. Look at the illustration on page 24. What's wrong here?

4. What did you learn about Homer by the end of the story? Explain.

"The Case of the Cosmic Comic"

Pre-reading/Motivational Activities:

1. Talk to the group about movie serials (for example, Superman).

2. Discuss these questions:
    What is a hero?
    What is a superhero?
    Do you have a favorite superhero? Who?
    How do you know your superhero isn't a real person?

Vocabulary;

cosmic (p. 34)
trick photography (p. 36)
chromium trimming (p. 41)
installment (p. 43)
barbed-wire (p. 46)

villain (p. 38)
stream-lined (p. 40)
monogram (p. 41)
modest (p. 45)
iodine (p. 47)

Questions:

1. Is Super Duper real to Freddy? How can you tell?

2. How is Homer's reaction to Super Duper different from Freddy and Louis' reaction to him?

3. Why do you think Freddy didn't want anyone to know about Super Duper's accident?

4. Why is Super Duper so popular when his adventures always turn out the same?

"The Doughnuts"

Pre-reading/Motivational Activity:

1. Discuss labor-saving devices. Ask students to give some examples. Discuss their pros and cons.

Vocabulary:

up-and-coming (p. 52)
frittered (p. 53)
chauffeur (p. 57)
pinochle (p. 62)
calamity (p. 63)
merchandising (p. 72)

automatic (p. 53)
"ride the rods" (p. 56)
gadget (p. 59)
tarnation (p. 63)
Zeus (p. 69)

Questions:

1. How are Homer and Uncle Ulysses alike?

2. What is the problem at the beginning of the story? Why does the problem get more complicated?

3. Which characters are most helpful to Homer? How are these characters alike?

4. Prediction: What do you think Homer might have done with all the doughnuts if the woman hadn't lost her bracelet in the batter?

"Mystery Yarn"

Pre-reading/Motivational Activities:

1. Ask students if they have or know someone who has a collection. Discuss why people become collectors.

2. Describe a county fair and the kinds of activities that go on there. If possible, look at some pictures of fairs.

Vocabulary:

leghorns (p. 77)
"carryings on" (p. 79)
pertaining (p. 83)
diameter (p. 85)
unprecedented (p. 87)

accomplished (p. 78)
spurn (p. 82)
maneuvering (p. 84)
rightful (p. 87)

86 / Homer Price

Questions:

1. How did Miss Terwilliger win the contest? (p. 94)

2. Was it fair? Why or why not?

"Nothing New under the Sun (Hardly)"

Pre-reading/Motivational Activities:

1. Read or tell about *Rip Van Winkle,* by Washington Irving, and *The Pied Piper of Hamlin,* by Robert Browning (*see* Related Books).

2. Discuss the meaning of "If a man can make a better mousetrap, the world will beat a path to his door."

Vocabulary:

concentrate (p. 100)
Ladies' Aid (p. 100)
speculate (p. 100)
antique (p. 104)
amnesia (p. 110)
deductions (p. 112)
compose (p. 115)
procession (p. 126)
crusade (p. 100)

new-fangled (p. 100)
blue-plate special (p. 103)
commission (p. 105)
individualist (p. 109)
complicate (p. 112)
deducting (p. 112)
impractical (p. 116)
torrent (p. 129)

Questions:

1. How was Michael Murphy like Rip Van Winkle and the Pied Piper?

2. How did the people judge Michael Murphy?

3. Why do you think the sheriff tried to cheat him?

"Wheels of Progress"

Pre-reading/Motivational Activities:

1. Discuss mass production and its effect on society.

2. Discuss the advantages and disadvantages of living in tract housing. If possible, show the group a picture of a tract community or home.

Vocabulary:

imperative (p. 134)	vicey versey (p. 135)
patent medicine (p. 135)	public-spirited (p. 136)
replica (p. 137)	mass-produced (p. 138)
assembly line (p. 139)	Woman Suffrage (p. 139)
receptive (p. 139)	union (p. 147)
arbitrate (p. 147)	compromise (p. 148)
picket (p. 148)	mercurochrome (p. 148)
pageant (p. 148)	modified (p.149)
tenants (p. 149)	commentator (p. 152)
formula (p. 152)	edible fungus (p. 153)
prosperity (p. 153)	quelled (p. 153)
symbolic (p. 156)	Grange (p. 156)
lynching (p. 157)	diagnosed (p. 157)

Questions:

1. Why were all the houses in Enders' Heights exactly alike?

2. Miss Enders decided to call the suburb Enders' Heights even though it was "flat as a board." Why do you think she chose that name?

3. Why do you think they changed the name of the town from Edible Fungus to Centerburg?

Questions about the book in general:

1. There is a great deal about progress in this book. What do the characters think they are progressing toward? What is the townspeople's vision of the future of Centerburg?

2. How are the people in the book like their names?

3. Look at the book's illustrations. How does the artwork reflect the text? Why do you think the artist chose to illustrate those particular events in the story? Which events would you have chosen to illustrate?

RELATED BOOKS

Ames, Lee Judah. *Fun-Time Radio Building*. Chicago: Children's Press, 1961.

Asimov, Isaac. *Words from the Myths*. New York: Houghton Mifflin, 1961.

Bartos-Hoppner, Barbara. *The Pied Piper of Hamlin*. New York: Lippincott, 1984.

Benjamin, Carol Lee. *Cartooning for Kids*. New York: Crowell, 1982.

Browning, Robert. *The Pied Piper of Hamlin.* New York: Frederick Warne, 1888.

_____. *The Pied Piper of Hamlin.* New York: Macmillan, 1987.

_____. *The Pied Piper of Hamlin.* New York: Rand-McNally, 1910.

Caney, Steven. *Steven Caney's Invention Book.* New York: Workman Publishing Co., 1985.

Goldberg, Rube. *The Best of Rube Goldberg.* Englewood Cliffs, N.J.: Prentice-Hall, 1979.

Hess, Lilo. *The Misunderstood Skunk.* New York: Scribner's, 1969.

Irving, Washington. *Rip Van Winkle.* New York: Macmillan, 1963.

_____. *Rip Van Winkle.* New York: Morrow, 1987.

McCloskey, Robert. *Blueberries for Sal.* New York: Viking, 1948.

_____. *Burt Dow, Deep-Water Man.* New York: Viking, 1963.

_____. *Centerburg Tales.* New York: Viking, 1951.

_____. *Lentil.* New York: Viking, 1940.

_____. *Make Way for Ducklings.* New York: Viking, 1941.

_____. *One Morning in Maine.* New York: Viking, 1952.

_____. *Time of Wonder.* New York: Viking, 1957.

Moss, Miriam. *Fairs and Circuses.* New York: Watts, 1987.

Murphy, Jim. *Weird and Wacky Inventions.* New York: Crown, 1978.

Pierce, Jack. *The State Fair Book.* Minneapolis, Minn.: Carolrhoda Books, 1980.

Robertson, Keith. *Henry Reed, Inc.* illus. by Robert McCloskey. New York: Viking, 1958.
    Other books in the Henry Reed series:
        Henry Reed's Baby-Sitting Service, 1966.
        Henry Reed's Big Show, 1970.
        Henry Reed's Journey, 1963.
        Henry Reed's Think Tank, 1986.

Schlein, Miriam. *What's Wrong with Being a Skunk?* New York: Four Winds, 1974.

Taylor, Barbara. *Weekly Reader Presents Be an Inventor.* San Diego: Harcourt Brace Jovanovich, 1987.

Weiss, Harvey. *How to Be an Inventor.* New York: Crowell, 1980.

ENRICHMENT ACTIVITIES

Homer Price

"The Case of the Sensational Scent"

1. Make a list of advertising slogans.

2. Do skunks make good pets? Research this question or interview an expert and share your findings with the group.

3. Find and read directions for building a radio. Tell the group what you learned about constructing radios.

4. Build a radio.

5. Write a script for the "robbers in bed and capture" scene on pages 24-28. Ask four friends to help you perform it for the group.

"The Case of the Cosmic Comic"

1. Make a Super Duper comic strip. Be sure to include smashing things, a rescue, and catching the villain at the end.

2. Have you ever seen or talked to a famous person (movie star, sports star, or politician)? Was this person different than you expected? Write a news article describing your experience.

"The Doughnuts"

1. Find a recipe for doughnuts and prepare it with an adult.

2. If possible, view a movie or videotape of "The Doughnuts." Compare the written version with the movie version. Which one did you like better? Why? Share your opinion with the group.

3. Create your own labor-saving device. Illustrate it, label its parts, and write a brief description of it.

4. Read page 72 for Uncle Ulysses' description of how the doughnut machine works. His words express the rhythm of the machine. Think of some other machine (blender, toaster, coffee pot, etc.), and write a poem that describes its rhythm and sound.

5. Brainstorm a long list of ways to use the extra doughnuts made by Uncle Ulysses' doughnut machine. List all of your ideas, no matter how silly some of them might sound.

"Mystery Yarn"

1. Do you have a collection? Bring your collection to school. Tell the group when you started collecting, why you started, and which items are your favorites.

2. Bring a ball of yarn to school. Have members of the group guess the length of the yarn. Make a list of their guesses. Measure the yarn to see who was the closest.

"Nothing New under the Sun (Hardly)"

1. Invent a better mousetrap. Draw a diagram of it and tell the group how it works.

2. Make up a tune that would attract mice. Perform it for the group.

"Wheels of Progress"

1. Find out how old your town or city is, what local events it celebrates, and how these events are celebrated. Make a poster advertising one of the events.

2. Draw a map of an imaginary town. Name the streets.

3. Design a costume for one of the spirits on page 156 (for example, the Spirit of Progress and Up-and-Comingness).

4. What is a spoonerism? (Hint: The sheriff uses them all the time.) Find some in the story. Make up some of your own.

5. Make a map of Centerburg.

6. Read *Centerburg Tales* by Robert McCloskey.

7. Create your own activity for one of the stories in *Homer Price*.

Jennifer, Hecate, Macbeth, William McKinley, and Me, Elizabeth

Author: E. L. Konigsburg

Illustrator: E. L. Konigsburg

Publisher, Date: Atheneum/Dell, 1967

Pages: 117

SUMMARY

An unlikely friendship begins on Halloween when Jennifer reveals to Elizabeth that she is a witch and that she is willing to take Elizabeth on as an apprentice. Elizabeth tells herself that witches don't really exist, but how else can she explain Jennifer's unusual behavior? This is a realistic novel about the problems and rewards of friendship.

PRE-READING/MOTIVATIONAL ACTIVITIES

1. Ask the students to read the title and look at the picture on the cover of the book. Ask them these questions:
    What do you think the story is going to be about?
    Who do you think the main characters are going to be?
    What do you think is the setting of the story?

2. Ask the students to make a list, together or individually, of all the things they know about witches. Read aloud the "Witch" entry in an encyclopedia. Ask the students to compare their list to the encyclopedia entry.

3. Before reading chapters 7-8, you might want to read a simplified version of *Macbeth* to students (*see* Related Books).

VOCABULARY/DISCUSSION QUESTIONS

Chapters 1-3:

Vocabulary:

caretaker's house (p. 3)
Cinerama (p. 5)
detention (p. 9)
quill (p. 15)
poetic license (p. 18)
apprentice (p. 26)
ceremony (p. 31)

estate (p. 4)
antique (p. 8)
two-faced (p. 13)
shawl (p. 17)
avalanche (p. 25)
DPT booster shot (p. 28)

Questions:

1. Why do you think Elizabeth hadn't noticed Jennifer at school before Halloween?

2. Why do you think Jennifer wore a paper bag on her head? (p. 16)

3. Why is Elizabeth so attracted to Jennifer?

4. Why does Elizabeth dislike Cynthia? (pp. 12-13)

5. How does Elizabeth know that the note on the tree was meant for her? (p. 24)

6. Why do you think Jennifer chose Elizabeth to be her apprentice witch?

7. Why do you think Jennifer always wears a skirt?

8. Make a list of everything we know from Jennifer about witches. (Add to this list after each section of the book is read and discussed.)

9. Is this a good friendship for Elizabeth?

Chapters 4-6:

Vocabulary:

colonial days (p. 36)
insectivorous (p. 36)
bubonic plague (p. 36)
ointment (p. 37)
cougar (p. 38)
indigo (p. 40)
frolic (p. 47)

Cotton Mather (p. 36)
guillotine (p. 36)
reputation (p. 37)
larynx (p. 37)
DDT (p. 39)
asafetida (p. 46)
dress rehearsal (p. 47)

(vocabulary continues on next page)

spontaneous combustion (p. 47)
Mona Lisa smile (p. 50)
picturesque (p. 51)
generations (p. 56)
precautions (p. 59)

Orlon (p. 47)
top billing (p. 51)
sarcastically (p. 54)
manufactured (p. 58)

Questions:

1. "After all, she had chosen me because she knew that I had all the makings of a fine witch." (p. 40) Why do *you* think Jennifer chose Elizabeth?

2. How does Elizabeth know that Jennifer is a "fine witch"?

3. Why is it so important to Elizabeth that Jennifer not be ordinary? (pp. 40-41)

4. Why do you think Jennifer and Elizabeth keep their friendship a secret? (pp. 44-45)

5. Why does Jennifer get so angry when Mrs. Stuyvestant calls her Jenny?

6. Why do you think Jennifer looks up when she is walking?

7. Is the Christmas week ritual (pp. 59-61) just a game to Jennifer and Elizabeth, or is it more serious than that? Explain your answer.

8. Do any of Jennifer's taboos for witches make sense? Why or why not? (pp. 76-77)

Chapters 7-8:

Vocabulary:

Brazil nuts (p. 74)
precautions (p. 76)
taboos (p. 76)
bobby pins (p. 84)
boa constrictor (p. 84)
deadly nightshade (p. 91)
Hecate (p. 96)

promotion (p. 76)
journeyman (p. 76)
cryptography (p. 79)
marionette (p. 84)
foxglove (p. 91)
Macbeth (p. 95)

Questions:

1. Is there any logical reason for the taboos to be grouped together on a list?

2. Why do you think Elizabeth doesn't tell her mother about Jennifer? (p. 80)

3. Why does Elizabeth enjoy herself at Cynthia's party?

4. Why do you think the toad meant so much to Elizabeth? (pp. 99-100)

94 / *Jennifer, Hecate, Macbeth, William McKinley, and Me, Elizabeth*

Chapters 9-10:

Vocabulary:

   invested (p. 103)   doused (p. 105)
   cauldron (p. 105)

Questions:

1. Why does the "flying ointment ritual" turn out as it does? What part does Jennifer play in the failure of the ritual? What part does Elizabeth play in the failure of the ritual?

2. Why isn't Elizabeth angry at Jennifer when she appears at her door?

3. Why do you think Jennifer takes the wagon everywhere she goes?

4. Why do the girls stop their witch game?

5. Why do you think the author named this book *Jennifer, Hecate, Macbeth, William McKinley, and Me, Elizabeth*? Is the order of the names significant?

6. Look at the book's illustrations. How does the artwork reflect the text? Why do you think the artist chose to illustrate those particular events in the story? Which events would you have chosen to illustrate?

RELATED BOOKS

Adler, David A. *Roman Numerals*. New York: Crowell, 1977.

Baron, Nancy. *Getting Started in Calligraphy*. New York: Sterling Publishing Co., 1979.

Byfield, Barbara. *The Book of Weird*. Garden City, N.Y.: Doubleday, 1973.

Jackson, Shirley. *Witchcraft of Salem Village*. New York: Random House, 1956.

Jennings, Gary. *Black Magic, White Magic*. New York: Dial, 1965.

Konigsburg, E. L. *About the B'nai Bagels*. New York: Atheneum, 1969.

_____. *Altogether, One at a Time*. New York: Atheneum, 1971.

_____. *The Dragon in the Ghetto Caper*, New York: Atheneum, 1974.

_____. *Father's Arcane Daughter*. New York: Atheneum, 1976.

_____. *From the Mixed-Up Files of Mrs. Basil E. Frankweiler*. New York: Atheneum, 1967.

_____. *(George)*. New York: Atheneum, 1970.

_____. *Journey to an 800 Number*. New York: Atheneum, 1982.

_____. *A Proud Taste for Scarlet and Miniver*. New York: Atheneum, 1973.

_____. *The Second Mrs. Giaconda*. New York: Atheneum, 1975.

_____. *Throwing Shadows*. New York: Atheneum, 1979.

_____. *Up from Jericho Tel*. New York: Atheneum, 1986.

McHargue, Georgess. *Meet the Witches*. New York: Lippincott, 1984.

Rackham, Arthur. *Tales from Shakespeare*. New York: Weathervane, 1975.

Snyder, Zilpha Keatley. *The Egypt Game*. New York: Atheneum, 1967.

_____. *The Headless Cupid*. New York: Atheneum, 1971.
  Other books about the Stanley family:
    The Famous Stanley Kidnapping Caper, 1979.
    Blair's Nightmare, 1984.

Starkey, Marion L. *The Tall Man from Boston*. New York: Crown, 1975.

ENRICHMENT ACTIVITIES

Jennifer, Hecate, Macbeth, William McKinley, and Me, Elizabeth

1. Write a plan for how to get more goodies on Halloween.

2. Read *The Tall Man from Boston* by Marion L. Starkey. Share some information about the Salem witch trials with the group.

3. Make a play out of the play described on pages 43-44. Perform it for the group.

4. What do you think the ingredients for flying ointment might be? Write your own recipe.

5. Draw a map of the community where the story takes place. Be sure to include William McKinley Elementary School, the library, the estate, the park, the woods, and Elizabeth's apartment building.

6. Get a book on calligraphy from your library. Collect the necessary materials and write a message using calligraphy.

7. Make a poster illustrating Roman numerals from 1 to 100.

8. Write a biographical sketch of Jennifer that tells all the background information about her that the book doesn't give the reader.

9. Write your own chant.

10. Read another book by E. L. Konigsburg.

11. Create your own activity for *Jennifer, Hecate, Macbeth, William McKinley, and Me, Elizabeth*.

Knight's Castle

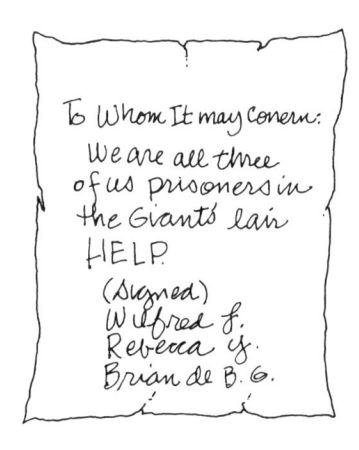

Author: Edward Eager

Illustrator: N. M. Bodecker

Publisher, Date: Harcourt Brace Jovanovich, 1956

Pages: 183

SUMMARY

Roger and Ann visit their cousins, Jack and Eliza, and are given an elaborate toy castle that they name Torquilstone after the castle in Sir Walter Scott's *Ivanhoe*. Fantasy becomes reality when Roger finds himself at the castle gate. The toy knights are real and so are the nighttime adventures of the four cousins. This humorous fantasy adventure story is a satirical look at knights and chivalry.

PRE-READING/MOTIVATIONAL ACTIVITIES

1. Provide the group some information about daily life during medieval times. Use books such as:
    Knights and Castles and Feudal Life by Alfred Duggan
    The Normans by Patrick Rooke
    The Saxons by Tony D. Triggs
    See Inside a Castle by Robert John Unstead
    The Time Traveler Book of Knights and Castles by Judy Hindley.

2. Ask the students to read the title and look at the picture on the cover of the book. Ask them these questions:
    What do you think the story is going to be about?
    Who do you think the main characters are going to be?
    What do you think is the setting of the story?

3. People often use quotes from television, books, and movies to express what they mean, for example, "make my day," "may the Force be with you," or "an eye for an eye." Explain to the group that the children in *Knight's Castle* use words and phrases from books that they have read and give some examples from the vocabulary lists below.

VOCABULARY/DISCUSSION QUESTIONS

Chapters 1-2:

Vocabulary:

yeomanly (p. 4)
terror to cats (p. 6)
few clouds to stir life's untroubled sea (p. 6)
all subterfuge failed (p. 7)
pining away (p. 10)
mean (frugal) (p. 11)
grenadiers (p. 13)
generations (p. 13)
skirmish (p. 14)
fray (p. 15)
by the rood (p. 15)
sundry (p. 17)
drawing room (p. 17)
industrial revolution (p. 19)
halidom (p. 19)
paltry striplings (p. 21)
pertinent (p. 21)
enthralled (p. 24)
tournament (p. 24)
turrets (p. 26)
portcullis (p. 26)
squires (p. 27)
ladies of high degree (p. 27)
chivalry (p. 28)
siege (p. 29)
simpering (p. 29)
henchmen (p. 30)
beseeching (p. 32)
parapets (p. 34)
foul churl (p. 35)
witless wight (p. 35)
shift (clothing) (p. 36)
sepulchral (p. 37)
wurra (p. 37)
gibbered (p. 38)
BVD (p. 39)
minion (p. 39)
Saxon (p. 39)
minikin (p. 40)
pennon (p. 43)

worms wouldn't endure (p. 5)
ruled with a rod of iron (p. 6)
back when the world was young (p. 6)
unrevealing (p. 8)
behindhand (p. 11)
draught (p. 11)
Spanish-American War (p. 13)
sentinel (p. 14)
murrain (p. 15)
plague (p. 15)
countenance (p. 15)
barbarous (p. 17)
flummery (p. 19)
sallied forth (p. 19)
gadzooks (p. 21)
wearisome (p. 21)
Ivanhoe (p. 24)
Knight Templar (p. 24)
suppressed (p. 26)
battlements (p. 26)
divers colors (p. 27)
pages (p. 27)
stalwart (p. 27)
jostling (p. 28)
ill-starred (p. 29)
languished (p. 30)
greensward (p. 30)
nobly (p. 32)
paltry knave (p. 34)
spurned (p. 35)
changeling (p. 36)
pardie (p. 36)
woe (p. 37)
hearken (p. 37)
garb (p. 38)
waxeth (p. 39)
hither (p. 39)
Norman (p. 39)
magazine (storage place) (p. 42)
parley (p. 43)

(vocabulary continues on next page)

Knight's Castle / 99

loitering (p. 44)
rue the day (p. 45)
varlet (p. 47)
cutting a swath (p. 47)
plateau (p. 48)

litter (stretcher) (p. 44)
colloquy (p. 45)
cleaved (p. 47)
thwart (p. 47)

Questions:

1. What do we know about Roger by the end of chapter 1? Be sure to include his age, his soldier collection, his feelings about the members of his family, and his imagination.

2. What do we know about Ann?

3. Why do you think Roger was intent on taking all of his soldiers with him to Baltimore?

4. What makes Roger think that the Old One is the "lucky charm of this family"?

5. The Old One tells Roger that wishes must be earned. How do you think Roger could earn his wish for his father's good health?

6. What are the "Words of Power"? Why do you think they are so powerful?

7. Prediction: Read the last two paragraphs at the end of chapter 2. What do you think is going to happen next?

Chapters 3-4:

Vocabulary:

glutting (p. 52)
suffice it to say (p. 58)
pox on it (p. 59)
trivet (p. 63)
sacrilege (p. 67)
utter melancholy (p. 71)
mollycoddle (p. 72)
poltroons (p. 77)
cuirass (p. 81)
Last Straw (p. 92)

mockery (p. 52)
ods bodikins (p. 59)
defied description (p. 62)
durance vile (p. 64)
sorceress (p. 69)
milksop (p. 72)
dastard (p. 75)
perfidious wretch (p. 81)
bane (p. 89)

Questions:

1. What convinces Roger that he should tell the others about his adventure? Why do the others believe him?

2. Why do you think Roger goes along with the girls' plan to modernize the city when he has said nothing but negative things about it?

100 / Knight's Castle

3. Why does Eliza like the city the way it is when she first arrives there? (p. 66) Why does she later think it's "perfectly disgusting"? (p. 70)

4. When Roger sees a knight riding in a motorcycle with his fair lady in the sidecar, he says, "It's sacrilege." (illustration on p. 50) What does he mean?

5. Who is the "mighty sorceress"? What spell did she cast? (p. 69)

6. The knights talk about Roger as if he is not an ordinary person (pp. 69, 79, 80). Who do they think he is?

7. Prediction: At the end of chapter 4 Ann wonders if the next adventure will be the last one. What do you think? Why?

Chapters 5-6:

Vocabulary:

   degenerate (p. 106)   gaffer (p. 106)
   pillion (p. 108)   beech-mast (p. 108)
   an arrow thrilled (p. 108)   caparisoned (p. 111)
   sustenance (p. 113)   jesses (p. 114)
   hobnobbing (p. 116)   ordeals (p. 119)
   bracken (p. 120)   carrion (p. 120)
   averted (p. 121)   Saracens (p. 122)
   impudence (p. 124)   atone (p. 128)
   quailed (p. 131)

Questions:

1. Reread the first two paragraphs on page 95. Why do you think the author capitalized "Had To Be" in the second paragraph?

2. Why are the knights playing baseball when Roger, Ann, and Eliza return to the castle?

3. How did Wilfred of Ivanhoe get to the Giant's Lair? Why do the children and the knights want to rescue him?

4. Why do you think the Black Knight is so happy to hear that Ivanhoe is back being knightly?

5. Why do Robin and Maid Marian find the appearance of the Giant's Lair so hideous?

6. How are dolls and knights different in their attitudes toward being played with? (pp. 133-134)

7. Why are the dolls so cruel to the knights?

8. Why do you think Jack is so dense about the "Words of Power"?

Chapters 7-8:

Vocabulary:

ploys (p. 140)
symbolic (p. 145)
lurk (p. 148)
sniffy (p. 155)
installment plan (p. 156)
cleaved (p. 161)
smidgin (p. 164)
balmy (p. 170)
prisoner's dock (p. 175)
durance vile (p. 178)

posterity (p. 143)
laggard (p. 145)
worst tyrant (p. 150)
on credit (p. 156)
false jade (p. 158)
rune (p. 168)
cutlery (p. 169)
contemptible (p. 175)
boon (p. 178)

Questions:

1. Why doesn't Jack's photograph turn out?

2. Why hasn't Roger told anyone about his secret wish? (p. 143)

3. Why doesn't the Old One just tell Roger what his task is instead of speaking in riddles?

4. When the children begin their quest to restore the dolls' missing belongings, Eliza decides that she will go with Roger and Ann will go with Jack. Why? (p. 146)

5. What kind of kingdom has the Leader set up? (chapter 7, beginning on page 147)

6. Why is Ann the one to figure out the rune?

7. Why does the Old One not speak until the end of the story? (p. 173)

8. How has Roger set the knights free and what has he set them free from?

9. Why is Roger's speech at the top of page 100 so admired by Robin Hood and the knights?

10. What is the Old One's role in each of the adventures? How is each of the things he does appropriate for his character?

11. Trace the history of the four children's friendship. How does their relationship change? Why?

12. Look at the book's illustrations. How does the artwork reflect the text? Why do you think the artist chose to illustrate those particular events in the story? Which events would you have chosen to illustrate?

RELATED BOOKS

Other books in the series:
Half Magic, 1954.
Magic by the Lake, 1957.
The Time Garden, 1958.

Other books by Eager:
Magic or Not?, 1959.
The Well-Wishers, 1960.
Seven Day Magic, 1962.

Berenstain, Michael. *The Castle Book.* New York: David McKay Co., 1977.

Clarke, Pauline. *The Return of the Twelves.* New York: Coward-McCann, 1963.

Cummings, Richard. *Make Your Own Model Forts and Castles.* New York: David McKay Co., 1977.

Goodall, John S. *The Story of a Castle.* New York: Margaret K. McElderry, 1986.

Gray, Elizabeth. *Adam of the Road.* New York: Viking, 1942.

Greer, Gery, and Bob Ruddick. *Max and Me and the Time Machine.* New York: Harcourt Brace Jovanovich, 1983.

Hindley, Judy. *The Time Traveler Book of Knights and Castles.* London: Usborne, 1976.

Little, Jane. *The Philosopher's Stone.* New York: Atheneum, 1971.

Lively, Penelope. *The Whispering Knights.* New York: E. P. Dutton, 1976.

MacCauley, David. *Castle.* Boston: Houghton Mifflin, 1977.

Mayne, William. *Earthfasts.* New York: E. P. Dutton, 1966.

Nesbit, E. *The Magic City.* New York: Coward, 1910.

Norton, Andre. *The Red Hart.* New York: Crowell, 1976.

Pyle Howard. *The Adventures of Robin Hood.* New York: Dover, 1968.

Rooke, Patrick. *The Normans.* London: Macdonald Educational, 1977.

Scott, Sir Walter. *Ivanhoe.* New York: Dodd, Mead, 1979.

Suskind, Richard. *The Crusader King: Richard the Lionhearted.* Boston: Little, Brown, 1973.

Sutcliff, Rosemary. *Knight's Fee*. New York: Henry Z. Walck, 1960.

_____. *The Shield Ring*. New York: Henry Z. Walck, 1956.

Triggs, Tony D. *The Saxons*. London: Macdonald Educational, 1979.

Twain, Mark. *A Connecticut Yankee in King Arthur's Court*. New York: Harper, 1899.

Uden, Grant. *A Dictionary of Chivalry*. New York: Crowell, 1968.

Unstead, Robert John. *Living in a Castle*. London: A & C Black (dist. Addison-Wesley), 1971.

_____. *See Inside a Castle*. New York: Warwick Press, 1979.

Vaughan, Jenny. *Castles*. New York: Watts, 1984.

Warwick, Alan R. *Let's Look at Castles*. Chicago: Whitman, 1965.

ENRICHMENT ACTIVITIES

Knight's Castle

1. Tape record a conversation between two or three people. Transcribe the conversation in yeomanly talk (for example, "Thou heardest me").

2. Read the scene on pages 71-75 as it is written. Select a portion of this scene and translate the yeomanly language into modern English. Present both versions to the group.

3. Make a model castle using the information from *Knight's Castle* or other books, such as *Castle*, by David MacCauley, or *See inside a Castle,* by Robert John Unstead.

4. Read *Ivanhoe* by Sir Walter Scott. Compare it to the version of *Ivanhoe* in *Knight's Castle*.

5. See the videotape of the movie *Ivanhoe* (1952) starring Robert Taylor. Have a discussion comparing the movie and *Knight's Castle*.

6. Read *The Adventures of Robin Hood* by Howard Pyle or another book about Robin Hood. Compare the portrayal of Robin Hood in *Knight's Castle* to the same character in another book.

7. Read *Half Magic, Magic by the Lake,* and/or *The Time Garden* by Edward Eager.

8. Read a biography of King Richard the Lionhearted (Richard I), and compare what you learn of his life with his character as portrayed in *Knight's Castle*.

9. Read another novel set in medieval times (*see* Related Books).

10. Learn more about the Normans and the Saxons. Who were they? Why were they at war? Report your findings to the group.

11. Create your own activity for *Knight's Castle*.

Mrs. Piggle-Wiggle's Magic

Author: Betty MacDonald

Illustrator: Hilary Knight

Publisher, Date: Lippincott/Scholastic, 1949

Pages: 126

SUMMARY

"Mrs. Piggle-Wiggle likes children, she enjoys talking to them and best of all they do not irritate her." She also has a shelf full of magic cures for their bad habits, ranging from bad table manners to tattletale-itis. This book contains eight Mrs. Piggle-Wiggle stories.

PRE-READING/MOTIVATIONAL ACTIVITIES/VOCABULARY/DISCUSSION QUESTIONS

"Mrs. Piggle-Wiggle's Magic"

1. Ask students to read the title and look at the picture on the cover of the book. Ask them these questions:
    What do you think the stories are going to be about?
    Who do you think the woman on the cover is?
    What kind of person does Mrs. Piggle-Wiggle seem to be?

Vocabulary:

gems (p. 1)   lapis lazuli (p. 2)
splotchy (p. 4)   bilious (p. 4)

Questions:

1. The first paragraph of this story says, "Mrs. Piggle-Wiggle likes children, she enjoys talking to them and best of all they do not irritate her." What makes this last quality "best of all"?

2. Why is Mrs. Piggle-Wiggle's response to Molly's problem with the dictionary such a good one? (pp. 1-2)

3. How is Mrs. Piggle-Wiggle different from parents?

106 / Mrs. Piggle-Wiggle's Magic

"The Thought-You-Saiders Cure"

Pre-reading/Motivational Activity:

1. Play "The Telephone Game" with the group: Whisper a sentence in one student's ear. Ask that student to whisper what you said into the next student's ear. Then ask that student to whisper the message into the next student's ear and so on. Ask the last student to get the message to tell the group the message. Compare this to what you said to the first student. The message will probably change a great deal as it is passed from person to person; the final version will probably be nonsensical. Discuss with the group why this nonsensical version of what you said is humorous.

Vocabulary:

groping (p. 8)
aggrieved (p. 8)
unison (p. 10)
mirth (p. 11)
ear trumpet (p. 11)
scuffling (p. 15)
talcum (p. 17)
slight (thin) (p. 18)
balefully (p. 23)

currant (jelly) (p. 8)
bannister (p. 9)
convulsions (p. 11)
paroxysm (p. 11)
corrupt (p. 14)
epidemic (p. 17)
spangled (p. 18)
agony (p. 20)

Questions:

1. Why do you think the children started "thought-you-saiding"?

2. How did the parents' and children's behavior change once the cure started?

3. What, besides magic, might have gotten them to stop?

4. Why do you think the artist put a picture of Abraham Lincoln above Darsie's bed?

5. At the end of the story Mr. Burbank says, "I thought you said, 'Go give Mrs. Piggle-Wiggle your hardest spanks.'" Is Mr. Burbank teasing or does he now have a case of "thought-you-said-itis"?

"The Tattletale Cure"

Pre-reading/Motivational Activities

1. Ask the students:
    What is a tattletale?
    How is a tattletale different from someone who is just reporting an incident?
    If you could see a tattletale, what would it look like?

Mrs. Piggle-Wiggle's Magic / 107

Vocabulary:

fragrant (p. 25)
evident (p. 26)
prig (p. 27)
flounced (p. 28)
kaleidoscope (p. 29)
ailment (p. 29)
sufficiently (p. 32)
unbearable (p. 33)

galoshes (p. 25)
horrid (p. 26)
loathsome (p. 27)
jostling (p. 28)
despise (p. 29)
maneuvering (p. 31)
well-nigh (p. 33)
suspended (p. 34)

Questions:

1. Why do you think Wendy tattles?

2. Why do you think Timmy tattles?

3. Both Wendy and Timmy are dressed in strange outfits after they are given the first dose of the cure. (p. 32) Do you think this is caused by the medicine, or is it just a coincidence? Explain.

4. Why does Wendy stop tattletaling?

5. Why do the indoor tattletales behave differently than the outdoor tattletales?

6. Do you think the cure is going to last? Explain.

"The Bad-Table-Manners-Cure"

Pre-reading/Motivational Activities:

1. Write "Bad Table Manners" on one side of the classroom chalkboard and "Good Table Manners" on the other side. Ask the students to list as many examples of each as they can.

2. Is it easy to have good table manners? Why or why not?

3. How do children learn good table manners?

Vocabulary:

pantry (p. 39)
whet the appetite (p. 41)
free rein (p. 42)
trough (p. 43)
indicate (p. 45)

assemble (p. 40)
compulsory (p. 41)
restricted neighborhood (p. 43)
misgivings (p. 44)
skeptical (p. 48)

(vocabulary continues on next page)

laundry (p. 49)
basin (p. 50)
quizzically (p. 53)
gluttonous (p. 54)

lavatory (p. 50)
flawless (p. 52)
unlatched (p. 53)
vigorously (p. 56)

Questions:

1. Why doesn't it do a speck of good for Mr. and Mrs. Brown to talk to Christopher about his manners?

2. Why do you think Lester winks at Mrs. Brown? (p. 45)

3. Why do you think Mr. Brown is so rude to Lester?

4. Why is it easier for Christopher to learn manners from a pig than from his parents?

5. Why is Christopher the one to notice that Mrs. Brown is serving Lester spareribs and bacon?

6. Do you think Lester was sad when he left the Browns? Why or why not?

"The Interrupters"

Pre-reading/Motivational Activities:

1. Ask five students to stand in front of the group and have each one talk about a different subject at the same time. After a couple of minutes, have them discuss how they feel about being interrupted or ignored by the other students.

2. Why do people interrupt other people when they are speaking? Give examples to support your opinions.

Vocabulary:

forsythia (p. 58)
rummaging (p. 61)
spectacle case (p. 65)
pinafore (p. 66)
stammer (p. 67)

indulgently (p. 59)
guarantee (p. 62)
drenched (p. 65)
sheepishly (p. 66)
rehash (p. 69)

Questions:

1. Why do you think Sally, Stevie, and Benji keep interrupting their parents?

2. Do you agree with Benji when he said that he thought his parents should have some powder blown at them, too? Why or why not?

"The Heedless Breaker"

Pre-reading/Motivational Activities:

1. Have students look up "heedless" in the dictionary. Ask them what they think a heedless breaker is.

2. Ask the students:
    Have you ever broken something that was very important to someone else? How did you feel? What did you do?

Vocabulary:

heedless (p. 70)
solicitously (p. 73)
buck saw (p. 76)
souffle (p. 78)
repentant (p. 78)
zeppelins (p. 78)
regally (p. 82)
warily (p. 85)

rimless spectacles (p. 73)
elocution (p. 75)
callously (p. 78)
delphinium (p. 78)
pruning (p. 78)
philodendron (p. 78)
knick-knacks (p. 85)

Questions:

1. Why do you think Sharon is a heedless breaker?

2. Why do you think Mr. and Mrs. Rogers react differently to Sharon's heedlessness?

3. Why is Mrs. Rogers *so* delighted when Mr. Rogers suggests calling Mrs. Piggle-Wiggle?

4. Mrs. Rogers is sure she won't need the magic powder anymore. What do you think? Why?

"The Never-Want-to-Go-to-Schooler"

Pre-reading/Motivational Activities:

1. Ask the students:
    What are all the reasons children might not want to go to school?
    What would happen to you if you didn't go to school?

Vocabulary:

chisel (p. 87)
ignorant (p. 88)

agony (p. 88)
amoebic dysentery (p. 88)

(vocabulary continues on next page)

hygiene (p. 88)
cartilage (p. 88)
frail (p. 90)
davenport (p. 90)
shinnied (p. 90)
heart-rending (p. 95)
invalid (p. 96)
earwig (p. 97)
mocked (p. 103)

hydrophobia kleptomania (p. 88)
esophagus (p. 88)
afghan (p. 90)
wistfully (p. 90)
meekly (p. 95)
vivid (p. 95)
high strung (p. 97)
perennial (p. 100)

Questions:

1. Why do you think Jody doesn't want to go to school?

2. Why do you think Mrs. Jones is so easily fooled by Jody?

3. When does Jody's ignorance start getting in his way?

4. What are the effects of the Ignorance Tonic?

5. How long do you think this cure is going to last?

"The Waddle-I-Doers"

Pre-reading/Motivational Activity:

1. Ask the students:
    When do children have a hard time thinking up something to do? What do *you* do in a situation like that?

Vocabulary:

pelting (p. 107)
scowling (p. 108)
compensation (p. 109)
surly (p. 114)
buffet (p. 117)

disconsolately (p. 108)
repose (p. 109)
mules (slippers) (p. 110)
territory (p. 117)
draughty (p. 123)

Questions:

1. Why do you think this is the only cure in the book with no magic?

2. This chapter is a mystery/treasure hunt. What are the clues?

3. Why does Mrs. Piggle-Wiggle take a nap in the middle of the search?

4. How does the rain bring both bad luck and good luck to the children?

5. Is Mrs. Piggle-Wiggle having a real emergency, or did she plan the treasure hunt for the children's entertainment?

Questions about the book in general:

1. Why do you think the author does not give Mrs. Piggle-Wiggle a first name?

2. Why do the minor characters often have such funny names (for example, Armand Armadillo) while the main characters do not?

3. Why do the mothers call other parents before they call Mrs. Piggle-Wiggle?

4. How does the form of the medicine suit the cure (for example, powder in the ear for the I-Thought-You-Saiders, powder on the sheets for the Heedless Breaker)?

5. Read the book's dedication. Do you think the stories' point of view is that of the children, the parents, or both?

6. Discuss how each of the cure stories has the same basic story elements. List them:
    a. The children have a bad habit that the parents can't break.
    b. The mother asks some other parent for advice.
    c. The mother calls Mrs. Piggle-Wiggle for help.
    d. Mrs. Piggle-Wiggle sends over a cure.
    e. The parents administer the cure and something happens to the children as a result.
    f. The children are cured.

7. Look at the book's illustrations. How does the artwork reflect the text? Why do you think the artist chose to illustrate those particular events in the story? Which events would you have chosen to illustrate?

RELATED BOOKS

Other Mrs. Piggle-Wiggle books:
   Hello, Mrs. Piggle-Wiggle, 1957.
   Mrs. Piggle-Wiggle, 1947.
   Mrs. Piggle-Wiggle's Farm, 1954.

Cooper, Elizabeth K. *And Everything Nice: The Story of Sugar, Spice, and Flavoring*. New York: Harcourt, Brace & World, 1966.

Travers, P. L. *Mary Poppins*. rev. ed. New York: Harcourt Brace Jovanovich, 1981.
   Other Mary Poppins books:
      Mary Poppins Comes Back, 1963.
      Mary Poppins in Cherry Tree Lane, 1982.
      Mary Poppins in the Park, 1952.
      Mary Poppins Opens the Door, 1943.

ENRICHMENT ACTIVITIES

Mrs. Piggle-Wiggle's Magic

1. Write a cure story of your own. Review the common elements of cure stories (*see* discussion question 6). Use this outline to write your story of an original cure for some problem behavior. You could use one of the problems in this book or make up a problem of your own.

2. Think of a cure for a parent's problem. Write a story about the problem, the cure, and the results.

3. Ginger appears many times in this book (gingerbread, ginger cookies, gingersnaps). What is ginger? Where does it come from? How is it used? Write a short report, bring some ginger to school, or make a recipe that calls for ginger.

4. Make cookies using gravy coloring instead of vanilla. What is the result?

5. Locate a book that tells about magic spells or alchemy. Share some of the information with the group.

6. Make a magic cure of your own. Be sure to include clear instructions on how the cure is to be used.

7. Design a lucky piece. Write a story about where you found it and why it is lucky.

8. Read another Mrs. Piggle-Wiggle book or another book about someone with magic cures for children (*see* Related Books).

9. Create your own activity for *Mrs. Piggle-Wiggle's Magic*.

Sadako and the Thousand Paper Cranes

> This is
> our cry,
> this is
> our prayer:
> peace
> in the world.

Author: Eleanor Coerr

Illustrator: Ronald Himler

Publisher, Date: Putnam/Yearling, 1977

Pages: 64

SUMMARY

Sadako Sasaki was a baby living with her family on the outskirts of Hiroshima when the atomic bomb dropped in 1945. Although she survived the blast, when Sadako was 11 she contracted leukemia. This book tells of her struggle to come to terms with the disease and the effect of her illness and death upon those around her. There is a monument to her and all other child war victims in Hiroshima's Peace Park.

PRE-READING/MOTIVATIONAL ACTIVITIES

1. Briefly discuss the time period of World War II, the fact that the United States was at war with Japan, and the awesome destructive power of nuclear weapons.

2. Read and discuss the book *Return to Hiroshima,* by Betty Jean Lifton, or another nonfiction book about the bombing of Hiroshima.

3. Locate Japan, Hiroshima, Nagasaki, Pearl Harbor, and the United States on a world map or globe.

4. Read *A Drop of Blood* by Paul Showers. This book describes what healthy blood is and what it does for our bodies. Discuss how leukemia changes healthy blood.

VOCABULARY/DISCUSSION QUESTIONS

Chapters 1-3:

Vocabulary:

    atom bomb (p. 7)
    Peace Day (p. 10)
    alter (p. 11)
    fidgeted (p. 11)

    radiation (p. 7)
    Oba chan (p. 11)
    memorial (p. 11)
    ancestors (p. 11)

(vocabulary continues on next page)

114 / Sadako and the Thousand Paper Cranes

leukemia (p. 13)
tatami mats (p. 14)
Buddhist priest (p. 18)
shrine (p. 26)

Hiroshima (p. 13)
ceremonies (p. 18)
kimono (p. 26)
throngs (p. 27)

Questions:

1. Why do you think Sadako was "always on the lookout for good luck signs?" (p. 10)

2. What kind of person is Sadako?

3. Why do you think Sadako doesn't tell anyone about her dizzy spells?

Chapters 4-6:

Vocabulary:

crane (p. 36)
parasol (p. 39)
blood count (p. 44)

omen (p. 36)
flustered (p. 44)

Questions:

1. Reread pages 34-36. Why did Chizuko bring Sadako a paper crane even though she herself didn't really believe in good luck charms?

2. Kenji was another leukemia patient at the hospital. How was his situation different from Sadako's? Why do you think the author introduced Kenji into the story?

Chapters 7-9:

Vocabulary:

wistful (p. 49)
blood transfusions (p. 56)

Questions:

1. Why do you think Mrs. Sasaki made Sadako a new kimono even though Sadako was near death?

2. Why didn't Sadako's parents tell her she was dying?

3. Aside from her illness, does Sadako change during the book? Explain your answer.

4. Why does the author begin and end the book with Peace Day?

5. Why do you think Sadako was chosen to be portrayed on the Peace Day monument to all children who were killed by the atom bomb? (p. 64)

6. Do you think this is a depressing or uplifting story? Why?

7. Look at the book's illustrations. How does the artwork reflect the text? Why do you think the artist chose to illustrate those particular events in the story? Which events would you have chosen to illustrate?

8. Read *Hiroshima, No Pika,* by Toshi Mareki, to the group. Preview the book because it is a very realistic picture of the destruction at Hiroshima. The book will raise many issues the children will wish to discuss. Compare the book to *Sadako and the Thousand Paper Cranes.*

RELATED BOOKS

Buck, Pearl S. *The Big Wave.* New York: John Day Co., 1947.

Caldwell, John C. *Let's Visit Japan.* London: Burke, 1965.

Davidson, Judith. *Japan, Where East Meets West.* Minneapolis, Minn.: Dillon Press, 1983.

Fradin, Dennis. *Radiation.* A New True Book. Chicago: Children's Press, 1987.

Gibbon, David. *Japan: A Picture Book to Remember Her By.* New York: Crescent, 1978.

Greene, Carol. *Japan.* Chicago: Children's Press, 1983.

Hawkes, Nigel. *Nuclear Energy.* New York: Watts, 1981.

Laurin, Anne. *Perfect Crane.* New York: Harper & Row, 1981.

Lifton, Betty Jean. *A Place Called Hiroshima.* New York: Harper & Row, 1985.

_____. *Return to Hiroshima.* New York: Atheneum, 1970.

Lowrey, Lois. *A Summer to Die.* Boston: Houghton Mifflin, 1977.

Mareki, Toshi. *Hiroshima, No Pika.* New York: Lothrop, Lee & Shepard, 1982.

Nakamoto, Miroko. *My Japan, 1930-1951.* New York: McGraw-Hill, 1970.

Pringle, Laurence. *Nuclear War: From Hiroshima to Nuclear Winter.* Hillside, N.J.: Enslow Publishers, 1985.

Say, Allan. *The Bicycle Man.* Boston: Houghton Mifflin, 1982.

Showers, Paul. *A Drop of Blood.* New York: Crowell, 1967.

Small, Fred. *Breaking from the Line: The Songs of Fred Small.* Cambridge, Mass.: Yellow Moon, 1986.

Stein, Conrad. *Hiroshima.* Chicago: Children's Press, 1982.

Weston, Reiko. *Cooking the Japanese Way.* Minneapolis, Minn.: Lerner, 1983.

Yagawa, Sumiko. *The Crane Wife.* New York: Morrow, 1981.

ENRICHMENT ACTIVITIES

Sadako and the Thousand Paper Cranes

1. Learn and perform the song "Cranes Over Hiroshima" (see *Breaking from the Line...* under Related Books).

2. Find out more about the significance of cranes in Japanese culture. Draw a picture of cranes and write a paragraph about their place in Japanese culture.

3. Locate directions for making origami cranes. Teach other members of the group how to make them.

4. Find out more about holidays in Japan, such as O Bon, New Year's Day and Peace Day. Write a paragraph about each holiday and share what you learn with the group.

5. Many Japanese foods were mentioned in the book. Look up recipes for one or two of these foods. Prepare samples of the food for the group.

6. Do a report on leukemia or the helpful and harmful effects of radiation.

7. Find out more about the atom bomb and the destruction it causes. Give an oral report to the group.

8. Survey 10 students to find out if they believe in lucky charms and if so, what kind they believe in and when they felt one worked for them. Write up the results to share with the group.

9. Write an original poem about Sadako.

10. Learn more about modern-day Hiroshima. What changes have occurred since the dropping of the atomic bomb on the city? Report this information to the group.

11. Create your own activity for *Sadako and the Thousand Paper Cranes*.

Song of the Trees

Author: Mildred D. Taylor

Illustrator: Jerry Pinkney

Publisher, Date: Dial/Bantam, 1975

Pages: 53

SUMMARY

The Depression has brought hard times to the Logans, a black family living in rural Mississippi. While Papa is away working for the railroad, an unscrupulous neighbor tricks Big Ma into selling him the beautiful stand of trees on the Logan farm. Papa returns, and the family finds a way to save the trees.

PRE-READING/MOTIVATIONAL ACTIVITIES

1. Discuss the realities of race relations in the South prior to the modern civil rights movement. Show the students photos that illustrate the institutional racial segregation that preceded the movement (*see* Related Books). Discuss the different experiences that black children and white children would have had at that time.

2. Discuss what life is like for poor families living in rural areas. Be sure to include reliance on homegrown food, transportation difficulties, limited job opportunities, limited public funds for education and public welfare, and a lower standard of living for everyone.

3. Ask the students to read the title and look at the picture on the cover of the book. Ask them these questions:
    What do you think the story is going to be about?
    Who do you think the main characters are going to be?
    What do you think is the setting of the story? (If students are unfamiliar wih the rural South, show them pictures of this part of the country.)

VOCABULARY/DISCUSSION QUESTIONS

Vocabulary:

kerosine/kerosene (p. 5)
canister (p. 5)
finicky (p. 6)
delved (p. 15)
resounded (p. 16)
"every which way but loose" (p. 24)
haggle (p. 29)
meddlesome (p. 45)
incredulously (p. 51)
sentries (p. 52)

clabber milk (p. 5)
laying tracks (p. 6)
sweet alligator gum (p. 11)
pine, beech, walnut, hickory trees (p. 16)
eerie (p. 19)
haughtily (p. 26)
venomously (p. 29)
ventured (p. 50)
ashen (p. 52)

Questions:

1. Who are the members of Cassie's family? Draw a diagram of the Logan family, listing the names and ages of each. (pp. 1-10)

2. What is Cassie's relationship to the trees? What is Stacey's relationship to the trees?

3. What is the first sign that something out of the ordinary is going on? Why do the trees become silent? (p. 19)

4. Read the middle of page 25 to the middle of page 29. How fair is the agreement that Mr. Anderson is trying to make? What does Mr. Anderson mean when he says, "You know, David might not always be able to work so good. He could possibly have . . . an accident"? Explain. (p. 25)

5. Why do you think the other family members do nothing about the trees while waiting for Papa to come home? (p. 33)

6. How did each of the children react to their father's confrontation with Mr. Anderson? (pp. 46-49)

7. What do you think Papa means when he says, "And it don't make me any difference if I die today or tomorrow. Just as long as I die right"?

8. What else does Papa say and do to convince Mr. Anderson that he is serious about blowing up the trees? (pp. 49-52)

9. Do you think the trees will ever sing again? Why or why not? (p. 52)

10. Look at the book's illustrations. How does the artwork reflect the text? Why do you think the artist chose to illustrate those particular events in the story? Which events would you have chosen to illustrate?

RELATED BOOKS

Other books about the Logan family:
Roll of Thunder, Hear My Cry, 1976.
Let the Circle Be Unbroken, 1981.
The Friendship, 1987.
The Road to Memphis, 1990.

Boyd, Candy Dawson. *Circle of Gold.* New York: Scholastic, 1984.

Clifton, Lucille. *The Lucky Stone.* New York: Delacorte, 1979.

Greene, Bette. *Philip Hall Likes Me, I Reckon Maybe.* New York: Dial, 1974.
Another Philip Hall book:
Get on Out of Here, Philip Hall. New York: Dial, 1981.

Hansen, Joyce. *The Gift-giver.* New York: Houghton Mifflin, 1980.

———. *Yellow Bird and Me.* New York: Clarion, 1986.

Mathis, Sharon Bell. *The Hundred Penny Box.* New York: Viking, 1975.

———. *Sidewalk Story.* New York: Viking, 1971.

Meltzer, Milton, and August Meier. *Time of Trial, Time of Hope: The Negro in America, 1919 to 1941.* New York: Doubleday, 1966.

Myers, Walter Dean. *Me, Mop and the Moon-Dance Kid.* New York: Delacorte, 1988.

Perl, Lila. *Red Flannel Hash and Shoo-Fly Pie.* New York: World, 1965.

Taylor, Mildred D. *The Gold Cadillac.* New York: Dial, 1987.

Walter, Mildred Pitts. *Justin and the Best Biscuits in the World.* New York: Lothrop, 1986.

———. *Mariah Loves Rock.* New York: Bradbury, 1988.

Yarbrough, Camille. *Cornrows.* New York: Coward, McCann & Geoghegan, 1979.

ENRICHMENT ACTIVITIES

Song of the Trees

1. Cook one or more of the dishes mentioned in the story. (*See Red Flannel Hash and Shoo-Fly Pie* in Related Books.)

2. The fourth and fifth paragraphs on page 2 describe the view outside Cassie's window in the early morning. She contrasts this view to the same view in full sunlight. Use watercolors to illustrate the two contrasting views.

3. The people in this story have differing attitudes toward the trees. To describe their differences graphically, make a continuum. Draw a horizontal line. At the left end, write, "Trees are beautiful and sacred." At the right end, write, "Trees are useful and expendable." With small vertical marks, divide the horizontal line into four equal parts according to their attitudes toward the trees. Write the names of the story characters on this continuum; write your own name on this continuum as well. Explain why you placed the names where you did.

Trees are beautiful   Trees are useful
and sacred.   and expendable.

|—————————|—————————|—————————|—————————|

4. At the end of the story Papa goes back to Louisiana to work on the railroad. Write a letter that Cassie might have written to Papa about the events following the confrontation with Mr. Anderson.

5. Find out more about racial segregation in the rural South in the early 1930s. Write a report focusing on the inequality that existed at that time.

6. Make a poster describing the trees found in Cassie's forest. (p. 16) Which ones are found in the area of the country where you live?

7. Read another book by Mildred D. Taylor.

8. Read another novel featuring African-American characters (*see* Related Books).

9. Create your own activity for *Song of the Trees*.

GRADE FIVE

The Egypt Game

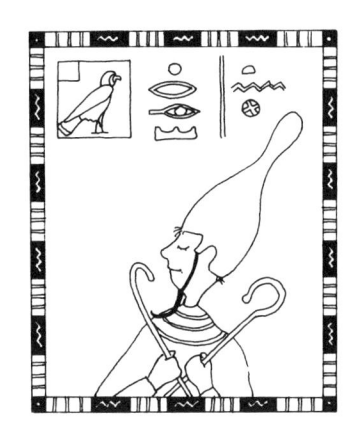

Author: Zilpha Keatley Snyder

Illustrator: Alton Raible

Publisher, Date: Atheneum, 1967

Pages: 215

SUMMARY

When 11-year-old April moves into the same apartment building as Melanie, the girls discover they have a common interest in imagining games and ancient Egyptians. The girls discover a discarded bust of Nefertiti in the hidden backyard of an antique shop, and the Egypt Game begins. This realistic novel is a suspenseful mystery.

PRE-READING/MOTIVATIONAL ACTIVITIES

1. Show the students a variety of books about ancient Egypt. Talk about how people have been fascinated by ancient Egyptians for hundreds of years for many reasons, including the many well-preserved artifacts and the amount of recorded information about their way of life.

2. Locate Egypt on a map of the ancient world.

3. Ask the students to read the title and look at the picture on the cover of the book. Ask them these questions:
    What do you think the story is going to be about?
    Who do you think the main characters are going to be?
    What do you think is the setting of the story?

VOCABULARY/DISCUSSION QUESTIONS

Pages 3-49:

Vocabulary:

    curios (p. 3)   gunnysack (p. 5)
    pert (p. 6)   Diana the Huntress (p. 7)

(vocabulary continues on next page)

Nefertiti (p. 7)
Korean War (p. 13)
pre-Columbian (p. 18)
Babylonia (p. 20)
reincarnation (p. 21)
"easy to snow" (p. 27)
escapades (p. 31)
monoliths (p. 35)
hieroglyphics (p. 35)
Isis (p. 45)

lotus blossoms (p. 8)
agent (p. 15)
dead-pan (p. 19)
archeologist (p. 20)
warily (p. 24)
vocalist (p. 27)
Nile (p. 34)
pharaohs (p. 35)
drastic (p. 39)
Set (p. 45)

Questions:

1. Why do you think most people are afraid of the Professor?

2. Why is the Professor interested in the children's game?

3. Why isn't April afraid of the Professor?

4. How does April feel about her mother? Her grandmother? How do they feel about her?

5. Why do you think April is so excited by "old stuff"? (p. 17)

6. Why does Melanie like April?

7. What does April mean when she thinks, "You never could tell with kids—they didn't do things in a pattern the way grown-ups did"? (p. 27)

8. What does Melanie mean by "imagining games"? (p. 32)

9. Why did Melanie's paper-doll game appeal to April? (pp. 30-31)

10. Why is Egypt fascinating to the girls? (pp. 34-35)

11. Why do you think Melanie is protective of April? (pp. 36-40)

12. Reread the first chapter. What is magic about the Egypt Game?

13. Why do you think the evil god Set grows "almost on his own and all out of control"? (p. 48)

Page 50-97:

Vocabulary:

papyrus (p. 55)
languishing (p. 68)
tunic (p. 75)
omen (p. 86)
unison (p. 96)

April is the cruelest month (p. 61)
remedial (p. 69)
token (p. 86)
demonstration (p. 90)

Questions:

1. April excuses Marshall's attachment to Security by saying, "Heck, I guess everybody has something they're not very grown-up about." (p. 58) Is there anything April is "not very grown-up about"?

2. Why is it so important that the Egypt Game be kept secret? (p. 62)

3. Why do you think the girls decide so quickly to let Elizabeth join the Egypt Game?

4. How did Elizabeth make the Egypt Game perfect? (p. 67)

5. Why do most people think the Professor is the murderer? Why don't the children think he is the murderer?

6. Why do you think the children couldn't play the Egypt Game indoors? (p. 74)

7. How is going to Egypt on Halloween "not at all like being downright disobedient"? (p. 82)

8. Why do you think Melanie agrees to go to Egypt even though she has so many misgivings about going? (pp. 84-85)

9. What kind of demonstration did Marshall think they were going to take part in? (pp. 90-91)

10. Do you think Melanie really sees a shooting star? (p. 96)

11. Prediction: What do you think will happen next?

Pages 97-158:

Vocabulary:

philosophically (p. 111)
Thoth (p. 124)
Ramose (p. 126)
Anubis (p. 133)
Ibis (p. 147)

non-violence (p. 113)
Bastet (p. 126)
Horemheb (p. 126)
oracle (p. 142)

126 / The Egypt Game

Questions:

1. What does Marshall mean when he says, "Somebody already has heard us"? (p. 101)

2. When the boys threaten to expose the game, Elizabeth says, "Please don't tell on us and we'll let you play, too." Why does this work?

3. Why does April think it is better to be mad than sad? (p. 118)

4. Why do you think Toby is so interested in the Egypt Game?

5. Why is Bastet especially appealing to April? (p. 126)

6. What does Toby add to the Egypt Game?

7. Why do you think the Ceremony for the Dead makes Ken less embarrassed about being an ancient Egyptian? (p. 140)

8. Why does Toby make such a point of keeping school life and Egypt separate? Do the girls agree? (pp. 144-145)

9. Does April really believe that the gods speak through the mouth of the priestess or is she just pretending? Explain.

10. Why is the game getting more frightening? Do the children like this development? Explain.

11. Prediction: How do you think the oracle really works?

Pages 159-215:

Vocabulary:

quotations (p. 168)   lair (p. 197)
seclusion (p. 197)   anthropology (p. 206)

Questions:

1. Why did Toby write answers for the oracle?

2. How are the children "a little like Dr. Frankenstein"? (p. 175)

3. Why don't the children want to try the oracle again? (p. 176)

4. Why do the children find magical explanations more compelling than practical explanations? (pp. 177-178)

5. Why does Marshall insist on going with April to Egypt to find her math book? (p. 180)

6. Why does Marshall shine the flashlight on the Professor's store window? (p. 183)

7. After Marshall becomes a hero, he leaves Security at home. Why? (p. 194)

8. Why is the chapter beginning on page 196 called "Gains and Losses"?

9. Why do you think April answers her mother's letter as she does? (p. 203)

10. What gift did the children give to the Professor? (p. 213)

11. If the Egypt Game had remained a secret, do you think the children would have kept playing it?

12. Look at the book's illustrations. How does the artwork reflect the text? Why do you think the artist chose to illustrate those particular events in the story? Which events would you have chosen to illustrate?

RELATED BOOKS

Aliki. *Mummies Made in Egypt.* New York: Crowell, 1979.

Allen, Kenneth. *One Day in Tutankhamen's Egypt.* New York: Abelard-Schuman, 1973.

Aylesworth, Thomas G. *Astrology and Foretelling the Future.* New York: Watts, 1973.

Cross, Wilber. *Egypt.* Chicago: Children's Press, 1982.

Glubok, Shirley. *The Art of Egypt under the Pharaohs.* New York: Macmillan, 1980.

Harris, Geraldine. *Gods and Pharaohs from Egyptian Mythology.* New York: Schocken Books, 1982.

Hawkes, Jacquetta. *Pharaohs of Egypt.* New York: Harper & Row, 1965.

Holmes, Burnham. *Nefertiti: The Mystery Queen.* London: Raintree Children's Books, 1977.

Katan, Norma Jean. *Hieroglyphs, the Writing of Ancient Egypt.* New York: Atheneum, 1980.

Macaulay, David. *Pyramid.* Boston: Houghton Mifflin, 1975.

Millard, Alan. *History in Pictures: The First Civilizations.* New York: Macmillan, 1979.

Millard, Anne. *Ancient Egypt.* New York: Warwick, 1978.

_____ . *The First Civilizations.* London: Usborne, 1977.

Neurath, Marie. *They Lived Like This in Ancient Egypt.* New York: Watts, 1965.

Pace, Mildred. *Wrapped for Eternity: The Story of the Egyptian Mummy.* New York: McGraw-Hill, 1974.

Perl, Lila. *Mummies, Tombs, and Treasure: Secrets of Ancient Egypt.* New York: Clarion, 1987.

Price, Christine. *Made in Ancient Egypt.* New York: E.P. Dutton, 1970.

Robinson, Charles Alexander, Jr. *Ancient Egypt.* rev. ed. New York: Watts, 1984.

Scott, Joseph, and Lenore Scott. *Egyptian Hieroglyphs for Everyone: An Introduction to the Writing of Ancient Egypt.* New York: Funk & Wagnalls, 1968.

Snyder, Zilpha Keatley. *And All Between.* New York: Atheneum, 1976.

_____. *And Condors Danced.* New York: Delacorte, 1987.

_____. *Below the Root.* New York: Atheneum, 1975.

_____. *The Birds of Summer.* New York: Atheneum, 1983..

_____. *Black and Blue Magic.* New York: Atheneum, 1966.

_____. *Blair's Nightmare.* New York: Atheneum, 1984.

_____. *The Changeling.* New York: Atheneum, 1970.

_____. *Eyes in the Fishbowl.* New York: Atheneum, 1968.

_____. *A Fabulous Creature.* New York: Atheneum, 1981.

_____. *The Famous Stanley Kidnapping Caper.* New York: Atheneum, 1979.

_____. *The Headless Cupid.* New York: Atheneum, 1971.

_____. *A Season of Ponies.* New York: Atheneum, 1964.

_____. *The Truth about Stone Hollow.* New York: Atheneum, 1974.

_____. *Until the Celebration.* New York: Atheneum, 1977.

_____. *The Velvet Room.* New York: Atheneum, 1965.

_____. *The Witches of Worm.* New York: Atheneum, 1972.

Unstead, Robert John. *Looking at Ancient History.* New York: Macmillan, 1959.

_____. *See Inside an Egyptian Town.* New York: Warwick Press, 1986.

ENRICHMENT ACTIVITIES
The Egypt Game

1. Make a map of the neighborhood in which April and Melanie live.

2. Make a scale model of a pyramid and the surrounding area.

3. Interview several children about favorite toys, blankets, stuffed animals, and similar items that they were attached to the way Marshall was attached to Security. Ask questions such as:
   How old were you when you got the object?
   How long were you attached to it?
   What happened to it?
   What conclusions about children and their special objects can you draw from these interviews? Write up your findings and conclusions.

4. Interview an antique dealer or collector. Find out why they are interested in old things, where they look for these things, what kinds of objects particularly interest them, and what got them started. Share the information with the group.

5. Research hieroglyphics. Make a poster showing common hieroglyphics and their translations. Include a message for others to translate.

6. Research Egyptian mummies and funeral rites. Write a report to share the information with the group.

7. Locate a book about Egyptian mythology. Choose an aspect that interests you and share what you learn with the group in one of the following ways:
   a. Learn a myth and tell it.
   b. Rewrite a myth as a play and perform it.
   c. Write and illustrate a report on a god or goddess.
   d. Design a costume for a god or goddess.

8. In the Egypt Game, the children play imagining games about the struggle between Isis (good) and Set (evil). Write your own story that includes the struggle between good and evil.

9. Read another book written by Zilpha Keatley Snyder.

10. Create your own activity for *The Egypt Game*.

Gone-Away Lake

Author: Elizabeth Enright

Illustrators: Beth Krush and Joe Krush

Publisher, Date: Harcourt Brace and World, 1957

Pages: 192

SUMMARY

Ten-year-old Portia and her younger brother, Foster, are spending a summer in the country with their cousin, Julian, and his parents. While Potia and Julian are exploring the nearby woods, they discover a row of abandoned summer houses on the shores of a swamp area that was once a lake. Two of the houses are occupied by a most unusual and interesting elderly brother and sister, Pindar and Minnehaha. The summer unfolds as Portia and Julian—and later, Foster—learn about nature and history as they enjoy a growing intergenerational friendship.

PRE-READING/MOTIVATIONAL ACTIVITIES

1. Show and discuss a filmstrip, video, or book that describes bogs and swamps.

2. Discuss what it means to "live off the land."

3. Ask the students to read the title and look at the picture on the cover of the book. Ask them these questions:
    What do you think the story is going to be about?
    Who do you think the main characters are going to be?
    Where do you think this story takes place?

VOCABULARY/DISCUSSION QUESTIONS

Plant Vocabulary:

pampas grass (p. 36)
pennyroyal (p. 52)
delphinium (p. 56)
pitcher-plant (p. 66)
arethusa (p. 67)
burdock (p. 136)
summer savory (p. 144)

angelica (p. 51)
horse balm (p. 52)
spagnum (p. 65)
sundew (p. 66)
wild cucumber (p. 136)
woodbine (p. 136)
bindweed (p. 145)

(vocabulary continues on next page)

orchis (p. 162)
cardinal flower (p. 162)
ironweed (p. 162)
joe-pye weed (p. 162)
boneset (p. 163)
elderberry (p. 163)
rose hip (p. 163)
Michaelmas daisy (p. 170)
Boston ivy (p. 170)

grass-of-Parnassus (p. 162)
lobelia (p. 162)
loosestrife (p. 162)
goldenrod (p. 162)
jimsonweed (p. 163)
hyssop (p. 163)
water hemlock (p. 163)
wild aster (p. 170)
monkey-puzzle tree (p. 184)

Chapters 1-4:

Vocabulary:

surfeited (p. 17)
airily (p. 27)
garnet (p. 29)
inconspicuous (p. 32)
turret (p. 33)
philosopher (p. 30)
leg-of-mutton sleeves (p. 37)
courtly (p. 38)
caprice (p. 43)
trousseaux (p. 46)
provisions (p. 46)
austere (p. 48)
kerosene (p. 48)
accentuated (p. 48)
entomologist (p. 50)
decoction (p. 52)

cowlicks (p. 17)
meteorite (p. 27)
caddis fly (p. 31)
voraciously (p. 33)
widows' walk (p. 33)
veered (p. 36)
pompadour (p. 38)
plundered (p. 43)
cataclysm (p. 44)
cherry mead (p. 46)
mandolin (p. 48)
baize (p. 48)
dapper (p. 48)
cyanide (p. 50)
decanter (p. 51)
deliberation (p. 55)

Questions:

1. " 'This car always smells exciting,' said Foster when they were inside it, and Portia knew just what he meant." (p. 20) What do you think he meant?

2. Portia has a reputation for being good at naming things. What does this say about the kind of person Portia is?

3. Why do you think Portia and Julian get along so well?

4. Why do you think Pin and Min decided to live at each end of the row of houses instead of next door to each other?

5. Why do you think Julian and Portia decide to keep Gone-Away Lake and Aunt Min and Uncle Pin a secret?

Chapters 5-8:

Vocabulary:

encroaching (p. 56)
hermetically sealed (p. 59)
eloquently (p. 61)
adenoids (p. 62)
pianola (p. 64)
damask (p. 69)
skulk (p. 72)
legions (p. 72)
buckaroo (p. 76)
sleight-of-hand (p. 78)
loathe (p. 87)
cribbage (p. 93)
tarpaulin (p. 100)
clamor (p. 101)
prudently (p. 105)
gloating (p. 106)

adornment (p. 59)
ingenuity (p. 61)
querulous (p. 61)
assertive (p. 63)
rheumatism (p. 69)
accessible (p. 71)
wheedled (p. 72)
lingo (p. 75)
buttonhook (p. 77)
conceded (p. 83)
laconically (p. 91)
sanctimonious (p. 96)
foible (p. 100)
guillotine (p. 105)
prefabricated (p. 106)

Questions:

1. " 'We plan to come every day, practically,' Portia assured her." (p. 68) What is so appealing about Gone-Away Lake?

2. When Tark comes back from school he is no longer Pin's best friend. (p. 73) Why do you think this happens? How does Pin turn this around? Why does Pin's plan work?

3. Why is Mr. Payton pleased when Portia and Julian decide to call their club the Philosopher's Club?

4. Read the text from the middle of page 107 to the end of page 108. What are the advantages and disadvantages of having friends that are old?

Chapters 9-12:

Vocabulary:

engrossed (p. 113)
ostentatiously (p. 123)
clothes-pole (p. 127)
subdued (p. 131)
spectacle (p. 131)
pontoon (p. 135)
condescend (p. 137)

expostulating (p. 119)
wince (p. 124)
cambric tea (p. 130)
conjectures (p. 131)
cravenly (p. 132)
plank and piling (p. 135)
amble (p. 143)

(vocabulary continues on next page)

schooner (p. 147)
imposing (p. 148)
runabout (p. 151)

chloroformed (p. 147)
landau (p. 151)
flounce (p. 152)

Questions:

1. How does the author set the scene for Foster to fall into the Gulper? Were you surprised when Foster got trapped in the Gulper? Why or why not?

2. How do the events of the day change Foster?

3. Why do Portia and Julian decide to invite more children to join the club?

4. Prediction: How is bridging the Gulper going to change Gone-Away Lake?

Chapters 13-15:

Vocabulary:

christen (p. 156)
proprietary (p. 158)
wrested (p. 166)
foliage (p. 167)
porte-cochere (p. 172)
callously (p. 174)
prophesied (p. 176)
placate (p. 179)
cryptically (p. 189)

officiate (p. 157)
intermittent (p. 161)
rueful (p. 166)
festooned (p. 169)
discordant (p. 172)
balustrade (p. 176)
transom (p. 176)
garrulous (p. 181)

Questions:

1. How is the house like Mrs. Brace-Gideon?

2. How is the relationship between Portia and Julian similar to the relationship between Minnehaha and Pindar? How is it different?

3. Look at the book's illustrations. How does the artwork reflect the text? Why do you think the artists chose to illustrate those particular events in the story? Which events would you have chosen to illustrate?

RELATED BOOKS

Cowing, Sheila, *Our Wild Wetlands*. New York: Julian Messner, 1980.

dePaola, Tomie. *The Quicksand Book*. New York: Holiday House, 1977.

Dunkling, Leslie. *The Guinness Book of Names*. Enfield, England: Guinness Books, 1986.

134 / Gone-Away Lake

Enright, Elizabeth. *The Four Story Mistake*. New York: Farrar, 1942.

———. *Return to Gone-Away*. New York: Harcourt, 1961.

———. *The Saturdays*. New York: Farrar, 1941.

———. *Spiderweb for Two*. New York: Farrar, 1951.

———. *Then There Were Five*. New York: Farrar, 1944.

Grimm, William C. *Indian Harvests*. New York: McGraw-Hill, 1973.

Martin, Alexander C., and Jean Zallinger. *Weeds*. New York: Golden Press, 1987.

Milne, Lorus J., and Margery Milne. *The Mystery of the Bog Forest*. New York: Dodd, Mead, 1984.

Pringle, Laurence. *Wild Foods*. New York: Four Winds, 1978.

Shuttleworth, Floyd S., and Herbert S. Zim. *Non-Flowering Plants*. New York: Golden Press, 1967.

Stone, Lynn M. *Marshes and Swamps*. Chicago: Children's Press, 1983.

Zim, Herbert S., and A. C. Martin. *Flowers: A Guide to Familiar American Wildflowers*. New York: Golden Press, 1950.

ENRICHMENT ACTIVITIES

Gone-Away Lake

1. Interview someone who has lived in your community for a long time (20-30 years). Find out about the changes that have occurred in the community. Write the interview as a news article.

2. Make a list of given (first) names from the story and a list of given names of the children in your group. Look up the names in a naming dictionary and note the meaning and derivation of each. Make a chart.

3. Min mentions medicinal plants in the story. Find out which common plants in your area are medicinal and make an illustrated chart of the plants and their uses.

4. Make a map of Gone-Away Lake and the surrounding area using the information in the story.

5. Locate some recipes that use wild foods as ingredients. Prepare one of them for the group (*see* Related Books).

6. Look up *alchemy* and *philosophers' stone* in a reference book. Share what you learn with the group.

7. Read *The Quicksand Book* by Tomie dePaola. Make your own quicksand using the directions in the book.

8. Read *Return to Gone-Away* by Elizabeth Enright.

9. Some people in Creston thought Min and Pin were crazy because they wore old-fashioned clothes and lived off by themselves. Do you agree or disagree? Write an opinion paper supporting your point of view.

10. Write a letter that Min might send to Portia during the winter following this story.

11. Draw a landscape of Gone-Away Lake, including many of the plants mentioned in the book. You will probably need to look the plants up in a plant identification guide.

12. Gone-Away Lake had changed from a lake to a swamp. Find out how and why this happens. Draw a series of pictures to illustrate how these changes take place.

13. Interview an antique collector to find out what is appealing about old things. Share the results of the interview with the group.

14. Create your own activity for *Gone-Away Lake*.

Harriet Tubman: Conductor on the Underground Railroad

Author: Ann Petry

Publisher, Date: Crowell, 1955

Pages: 221

SUMMARY

This is a biography of Harriet Tubman, the remarkable woman who was born a slave in Maryland, escaped to the North by way of the Underground Railroad, and went on to become known as "the Moses of her people," leading over 300 slaves to freedom. Her story is skillfully interwoven with other events and people of the 1800s.

PRE-READING/MOTIVATIONAL ACTIVITIES

1. Discuss the institution of slavery in the United States. Be sure to include when African slaves were first brought to North America; the kind of work they did; the conditions in which they lived; regions in which slaves were owned, and why; the existence of free black people in the United States; and the attitudes of various people toward slaves and slavery. Look at pictures of plantations, slaves quarters, and so forth in books such as *A Pictorial History of Black Americans* by Langston Hughes, et al. (*see* Related Books).

2. Locate Maryland on a map of the eastern United States. On a map of Maryland locate Chesapeake Bay, Dorchester County, Bucktown, and the Choptank River.

3. Make a list of words and phrases summarizing what the group knows about the Underground Railroad. Refer to the list and add to it as you read the book.

VOCABULARY/DISCUSSION QUESTIONS

People mentioned in the book:

Thomas Garrett and Sarah Garrett (p. 2)
Denmark Vesey (p. 14)
Mingo Harth (p. 15)
Thomas Jefferson (p. 27)
John Russwurm (p. 44)
Tice Davids (p. 47)
Nat Turner (p. 49)

John Brown (p. 2)
Peter Poyas (p. 15)
Theodore Parker (p. 18)
Henry Clay (p. 34)
Reverend Samuel Cornish (p. 44)
Reverend John Rankin (p. 48)
Phillip Bolling (p. 52)

(vocabulary continues on next page)

Harriet Tubman: Conductor on the Underground Railroad / 137

Henry Berry (p. 53)
John Hunn (p. 80)
J. Miller McKim (p. 95)
Daniel Webster (p. 105)
Millard Fillmore (p. 111)
Thomas Sims (p. 114)
Reverend J. W. Loguen (p. 118)
Charles Wheaton (p. 118)
William H. Seward (p. 118)
Frederick Douglass (p. 128)
Stephen Douglas (p. 140)
Edward G. Loring (p. 141)
Chief Justice Roger B. Taney (p. 181)
Abraham Lincoln (p. 182)
Franklin B. Sanborn (p. 183)
Thomas Wentworth Higginson (p. 183)
Levi Coffin (p. 195)
John A. Andrews (p. 200)
Sergeant Prince Rivers (p. 204)
General David Hunter (p. 209)
Ulysses Grant (p. 210)
Sarah Hopkins Bradford (p. 213)
Samuel Miles Hopkins (p. 214)

William Lloyd Garrison (p. 63)
William Still (p. 95)
John C. Calhoun (p. 105)
Reverend Theodore Parker (p. 111)
Shadrach (p. 114)
George Ticknor Curtis (p. 115)
Samuel May (p. 118)
Gerrit Smith (p. 118)
William Craft and Ellen Craft (p. 127)
Harriet Beecher Stowe (p. 134)
Anthony Burns (p. 141)
James Buchanan (p. 181)
Dred Scott (p. 181)
Molly Pitcher (p. 183)
Wendell Phillips (p. 183)
Amelia Bloomer (p. 190)
Charles Nalle (p. 196)
Jefferson Davis (p. 201)
Col. James Montgomery (p. 204)
Henry K. Durrant (p. 209)
John Wilkes Booth (p. 211)
Nelson Davis (p. 213)
Col. Robert Gould Shaw (p. 216)

Chapters 1-6:

Vocabulary:

conductor (title)
Chesapeake Bay (p. 1)
ebb and flow (p. 1)
Dorchester County (p. 1)
planter (p. 1)
hostlers (p. 2)
chinks (p. 2)
clay-daubed (p. 3)
basket name (pet name) (p. 4)
manumit (manumission) (p. 6)
gunning skiffs (p. 8)
prime (field hands) (p. 9)
Missouri Compromise (p. 9)
bandanna (p. 11)
assuaged (p. 13)
insurrection (p. 14)
Book of Zechariah (p. 14)
pikes (weapon) (p. 15)

Underground Railroad (title)
Tidewater Maryland (p. 1)
plantation (p. 1)
Big Buckwater River (p. 1)
letters of introduction (p. 2)
cultivated land (p. 2)
roughhewn (p. 3)
sway-backed (p. 3)
chain gang (p. 6)
Choptank River (p. 8)
punts (p. 8)
overseer (p. 9)
pork rind (p. 11)
Middle Passage (p. 12)
degrading (p. 14)
Charleston, South Carolina (p. 14)
Old Testament (p. 14)
uprising (p. 15)

(vocabulary continues on next page)

conspirators (p. 15)	servile (p. 16)
bondage (p. 16)	surreptitiously (p. 17)
North Star (p. 20)	prophesy (p. 21)
Moses (p. 22)	children of Israel (p. 22)
tow-linen (p. 23)	curative power (p. 32)
bronchitis (p. 32)	timbre (p. 32)
intractable (p. 34)	New Orleans (p. 37)
Natchez (p. 37)	coffle (p. 37)
interminable (p. 42)	orrisroot (p. 42)
hog wallow (p. 45)	refractory (p. 47)
Quakers (p. 48)	Methodists (p. 48)
prophet (p. 50)	visions (p. 50)
militia (p. 50)	Federal troops (p. 50)

Questions:

1. Make a list of the arguments given by slaves for and against running away to the North. Discuss the merits of each argument.

2. How could such an effective communication system exist between slaves? Why do you think the masters found it both amusing and disturbing? (pp. 8-9)

3. Why were young slave children not fed and clothed adequately?

4. Why did most of the slaves "fear change"? (p. 17)

5. How did Denmark Vesey's insurrection cause problems for the other slaves? In the long run, how did it help them? (pp. 14-18)

6. Even though she had no formal education, Harriet learned a great deal as she grew up. What was she taught and why?

7. Why do you think Old Rit found Harriet's "hiring out" to the Cooks so disturbing?

8. Why was the term Underground Railroad especially suited to describe the system that helped fugitive slaves escape to the North?

9. Read the Henry Berry quote on page 53. Tell what the quote means in your own words.

Chapters 7-11:

Vocabulary:

cornhusking bee (p. 54)	propitiation (p. 55)
desultorily (p. 56)	conjure (p. 58)
stupor (p. 58)	sixpence (p. 60)

(vocabulary continues on next page)

Harriet Tubman: Conductor on the Underground Railroad / 139

inertness (p. 60)
conscience-stricken (p. 63)
audacity (p. 66)
irradicable (p. 67)
trousseau (p. 74)
lying fallow (p. 75)
inconsolable (p. 91)
stringent (p. 93)
Philadelphia (p. 94)
Lebanon Seminary (p. 95)
dinghy (p. 102)
harboring slaves (p. 104)

coma (p. 60)
administer (p. 64)
diminutives (p. 66)
Boston (p. 71)
dilapidated (p. 75)
Wilmington, Delaware (p. 80)
guttural speech (p. 92)
fugitive slave laws (p. 93)
Vigilance Committee (p. 95)
talisman (p. 100)
undercurrent (p. 104)
Abolitionists (p. 105)

Questions:

1. Why do you think the masters gave the slaves a holiday?

2. Why did Harriet risk so much to help Barrett's slave escape?

3. Why do you think Harriet was so remorseful when she thought her prayers had caused the Master's death? (pp. 64-65)

4. How was making the patchwork quilt "the hardest task she (Harriet) had ever undertaken"? (p. 73)

5. Why do you think Harriet looked up to John Tubman?

6. Why did John Tubman refuse to help Harriet run away?

7. Why did Harriet take the patchwork quilt with her? Why do you think she left it with the woman who hid her on the first night?

8. What made Harriet decide to go back to Maryland and help other slaves escape?

Chapters 12-17:

Vocabulary:

retrospect (p. 110)
infidelity (p. 112)
Liberty Party (p. 116)
religious ardor (p. 117)
whippoorwill (p. 120)
mutinous (p. 127)
eloquence (p. 128)
fastidious (p. 132)

gaoling (p. 111)
impromptu (p. 112)
prodigious (p. 117)
prescience (p. 117)
disheveled (p. 123)
rheumatism (p. 128)
indomitable (p. 130)
St. Catherines, Ontario (p. 132)

(vocabulary continues on next page)

cryptic (p. 136)
Kansas-Nebraska Bill (p. 141)
fodder house (p. 144)
propaganda (p. 137)
ramshackle (p. 144)
pretensions (p. 151)

Questions:

1. "Her (Harriet's) mind, her soul, would always wear freedom's clothes. John's never would." (p. 110) What does the author mean by this?

2. Following her unsuccessful attempt to help John Tubman escape, Harriet "developed a much broader purpose" for her involvement in the Underground Railroad. (p. 112) What was this purpose?

3. Why did Harriet Tubman become such a legend?

4. Why do you think Harriet was never captured on one of her trips to Maryland?

5. Why do you think she made only two trips to Maryland each year?

Chapters 18-22:

Vocabulary:

inauspiciously (p. 156)
nostalgia (p. 178)
mortgage (p. 179)
Faneuil Hall (p. 185)
opium (p. 186)
Boston Common (p. 189)
missionary (p. 190)
Harper's Ferry (p. 191)
scaffold (p. 193)
martyr (p. 193)
seceded (p. 200)
warmonger (p. 201)
contrabands (p. 202)
concoction (p. 203)
detachment (p. 204)
ratification (p. 211)
remuneration (p. 211)
tuberculosis (p. 213)
epitomize (p. 217)
Gullahs (p. 217)
era (p. 220)

paregoric (p. 168)
Auburn, New York (p. 178)
daguerreotypes (p. 183)
reticule (p. 185)
environs (p. 188)
aired their grievances (p. 190)
arsenal (p. 191)
gallows (p. 193)
felon (p. 193)
woman's suffrage (p. 198)
militia (p. 201)
Confederate States of America (p. 201)
dysentery (p. 203)
draw rations (p. 203)
sagacity (p. 207)
Thirteenth Amendment to the Constitution (p. 211)
haversack (p. 211)
pension (p. 214)
tremulous (p. 217)
decipherable (p. 217)

Harriet Tubman: Conductor on the Underground Railroad / 141

Questions:

1. Why did Harriet wait such a long time to bring Old Rit and Ben north?

2. How was carrying live chickens an effective disguise? (p. 169)

3. What do you think made Harriet a "tremendously successful public speaker"? (p. 189)

4. Why did she trust John Brown enough to give him maps of her hiding places?

5. Do you think Harriet would have helped John Brown if she had known his purpose?

6. What does the author mean when she says, "He (John Brown) became a ghost and a legend that haunted both North and South"? (p. 92)

7. How can a person's influence extend beyond death?

8. Reread the excerpts from Abraham Lincoln's speech in Hartford, Conn., on pages 207-208. Explain in your own words what he meant when he said, "The same amount of property would have an equal influence upon us if owned in the North. Human nature is the same—people at the South are the same as those at the North, barring the difference in circumstances. . . ."

9. Why do you think a woman of Harriet Tubman's stature would have such a difficult time making a living?

10. What does the author mean when she says, "In many ways she (Harriet Tubman) represented the end of an era, the most dramatic, and the most tragic, era in American history." (p. 220)

11. Why do you think the inscription on the city of Auburn's memorial to Harriet Tubman is written in dialect? (pp. 220-221)

RELATED BOOKS

Archer, Jules. *Angry Abolitionist: William Lloyd Garrison.* New York: Julian Messner, 1969.

Bisson, Terry. *Nat Turner: Slave Revolt Leader.* New York: Chelsea House, 1988.

Borzendowski, Janice. *John Russwurm.* New York: Chelsea House, 1989.

Buchmaster, Henrietta. *Flight to Freedom: The Story of the Underground Railroad.* New York: Crowell, 1958.

Chapman, Abraham, ed. *Steal Away: Stories of the Runaway Slaves.* New York: Praeger, 1971.

Evitts, William J. *Captive Bodies, Free Spirits: The Story of Southern Slavery.* New York: Julian Messner, 1985.

Faber, Doris. *I Will Be Heard: The Life of William Lloyd Garrison*. New York: Lothrop, Lee & Shepard, 1970.

Freedman, Florence B. *Two Tickets to Freedom: The True Story of Ellen and William Craft, Fugitive Slaves*. New York: Simon & Schuster, 1971.

Goldston, Robert. *The Coming of the Civil War*. New York: Macmillan, 1972.

Goodman, Walter. *Black Bondage: The Life of Slaves in the South*. New York: Farrar, Straus, Giroux, 1969.

Graham, Lorenz. *John Brown: A Cry for Freedom*. New York: Crowell, 1980.

Greene, Carla. *Moses, the Great Lawgiver*. Irvington-on-Hudson, N.Y.: Harvey House, 1968.

Griffin, Judith Berry. *Nat Turner*. New York: Coward, McCann & Geoghegan, 1970.

Hamilton, Virginia. *Anthony Burns: The Defeat and Triumph of a Fugitive Slave*. New York: Knopf, 1988.

Hughes, Langston, Milton Meltzer, and C. Eric Lincoln. *A Pictorial History of Black Americans*. New York: Crown, 1973.

Iger, Eve Marie. *John Brown: His Soul Goes Marching On*. New York: Young Scott Books, 1969.

Ingraham, Leonard. *Slavery in the United States*. New York: Watts, 1968.

Jakoubek, Robert. *Harriet Beecher Stowe*. New York: Chelsea House, 1989.

Johnston, Johanna. *Harriet and the Runaway Book: The Story of Harriet Beecher Stowe and Uncle Tom's Cabin*. New York: Harper & Row, 1977.

Katz, William Loren. *An Album of Reconstruction*. New York: Watts, 1974.

_____. *An Album of the Civil War*. New York: Watts, 1974.

_____. *Slavery to Civil War. 1812-1865 Minorities in American History*. vol. 2. New York: Watts, 1974.

Killens, John Oliver. *Great Gettin' Up Morning: A Biography of Denmark Vesey*. Garden City, N.Y.: Doubleday, 1972.

Klagsbrun, Francine. *Freedom Now! The Story of the Abolitionists*. Boston: Houghton Mifflin, 1972.

Latham, Frank B. *The Dred Scott Decision, March 6, 1857*. New York: Watts, 1968

Lawrence, Jacob. *Harriet and the Promised Land*. New York: Windmill/Simon & Schuster, 1968.

Lester, Julius. *To Be a Slave*. New York: Dial, 1968.

Meltzer, Milton. *All Times, All Peoples: A World History of Slavery*. New York: Harper & Row, 1980.

Petersham, Maud, and Miska Petersham. *Moses*. New York: Macmillan, 1958.

Petry, Ann. *Tituba of Salem Village*. New York: Crowell, 1964.

Russell, Sharman Apt. *Frederick Douglass: Abolitionist Editor*. New York: Chelsea House, 1988.

Saporta, Raphael. *A Basket in the Reeds*. Minneapolis, Minn.: Lerner, 1965.

Scott, John Anthony. *Hard Trials on My Way: Slavery and the Struggle Against It, 1800-1860*. New York: Knopf, 1974.

Stein, R. Conrad. *The Story of the Underground Railroad*. Chicago: Children's Press, 1981.

Stowe, Harriet Beecher. *Uncle Tom's Cabin*. New York: Coward, McCann & Geoghegan, 1929.

ENRICHMENT ACTIVITIES

Harriet Tubman: Conductor on the Underground Railroad

1. Make and label a map of the Brodas plantation.

2. Research the life of the biblical Moses. How is Harriet's life similar to his? Make a chart comparing their lives and achievements.

3. Research one or more of the following topics:
    Fugitive slave laws
    Dred Scott decision
    Missouri Compromise
    Kansas-Nebraska Bill
    Boston Common incident
    Uncle Tom's Cabin by Harriet Beecher Stowe
    Harper's Ferry incident

4. If you are in an area where a station on the Underground Railroad was once located, find out as much as you can about it and share this information with the group.

5. Review chapter 15. Trace the route taken by Harriet Tubman from Dorchester County, Md., to St. Catherines, Ont., on an outline map of the northeastern United States and southeastern Canada.

6. "Freedom's a hard-bought thing, not bought with dust, but bought with all of oneself—the bones, the spirit and the flesh—and once obtained it had to be cherished, no matter what the cost." (p. 153) Write an essay describing your thoughts on this subject.

7. Write a log that a fugitive slave might have written while traveling on the Underground Railroad with Harriet Tubman.

8. Ann Petry mentions many people besides Harriet Tubman who worked for the abolition of slavery. Locate and read a biography of one or more of the following people and write a report focusing on their contributions to the antislavery movement.

Denmark Vesey	Nat Turner
John Brown	William Lloyd Garrison
William Craft and Ellen Craft	Frederick Douglass
Harriet Beecher Stowe	Anthony Burns
Thomas Wentworth Higginson	Levi Coffin
Thomas Garrett and Sarah Garrett	Theodore Parker
William H. Seward	John Russwurm

9. Research the Abolitionist Movement. Find out how it started, who were among the earliest abolitionists, what caused the movement grow, and what effect the movement had on the institution of slavery in this country. Share the information with the group.

10. Read another book by Ann Petry.

11. Design a wanted poster for Harriet Tubman. Use details from the book to make your poster as realistic as possible.

12. Make a quilt square. Use a traditional pattern or create a design of your own.

13. Ask many students of various ages what they think the Underground Railroad was. Organize and graph the information.

14. Research the lives of free black people in the United States before the Civil War. Share your information with the group.

15. Create your own activity for *Harriet Tubman: Conductor on the Underground Railroad.*

In the Year of the Boar and Jackie Robinson

Author: Bette Bao Lord

Illustrator: Marc Simont

Publisher, Date: Harper & Row, 1984

Pages: 169

SUMMARY

The story begins in China as eight-year-old Shirley Wong and her mother learn that they soon will be moving to the United States to join her father in New York City. Shirley's first year in the United States is the Chinese Year of the Boar. It is also the exciting year that Jackie Robinson and the Brooklyn Dodgers go to the World Series. Although the two cultures are very different, Shirley manages to create her own identity as both a Chinese and an American.

PRE-READING/MOTIVATIONAL ACTIVITIES

1. Shirley moved from China to New York in the late 1940s. Show the group pictures of China (circa 1940) and pictures of brownstone apartments in New York City. Discuss how life might be different in the two places.

2. Discuss the Chinese calendar.

3. Explain the process for emigrating from one country to another. Discuss reasons why people might want to do this.

4. Talk about who Jackie Robinson was and summarize the important contributions that he made.

5. Ask the students to read the title and look at the picture on the cover of the book. Ask them these questions:
    What do you think the story is going to be about?
    Who do you think the main characters are going to be?
    What do you think is the setting of the story?

VOCABULARY/DISCUSSION QUESTIONS

Chapter 1:

Vocabulary:

Confucian family (p. 2)
Patriarch (p. 2)
brazier (p. 4)
Matriarch (p. 7)
buddha (p. 9)
clan (p. 13)
ancestor (p. 15)

elders (p. 2)
cleaver (p. 3)
jade (p. 5)
dictums (p. 7)
abacus (p. 9)
mah-jongg (p. 14)

Questions:

1. What is a bandit? (Discuss good and bad associations with the word.) Why do you think Bandit was called by that name? What does this tell us about her?

2. How does Bandit feel about leaving China and going to the United States?

3. Use the information in chapter 1 to draw a family tree for Bandit's extended family.

Chapter 2:

Vocabulary:

writhe/writhed (p. 21)
cringe (p. 22)
dapper (p. 25)
attained (p. 29)
replica (p. 33)
rebuke (p. 39)

unique (p. 22)
engineer (p. 24)
ogled (p. 26)
"prove her mettle" (p. 32)
skeptical (p. 34)

Questions:

1. "Home was Brooklyn, New York, but Shirley would not know that for a while. To her, it was simply Mei Guo, Beautiful Country." (p. 26) What do you think Shirley found beautiful about Brooklyn?

2. What was Shirley's family's social/economic status in China? How does that change when they move to New York?

3. "Then, a wonderful idea popped into Shirley's head. She would go for the cigarettes." (p. 34) Why does Shirley insist on going to the store for cigarettes by herself?

148 / In the Year of the Boar and Jackie Robinson

4. Why do you think Shirley's father decided to emigrate to the United States? Find evidence in the story to support your opinion.

5. Trace Shirley and her mother's "journey of ten thousand miles" from China to New York City on a globe or wall map.

Chapters 3-4:

Vocabulary:

ambassador (p. 41)
foreign/foreigner (p. 42)
gesture (p. 44)
Kwan Yin, Goddess of Mercy (p. 47)
tic (p. 52)
delicatessen (p. 53)
humiliated (p. 58)
hoary (p. 58)
odious (p. 58)
eked (p. 59)
fluently (p. 64)

P.S. 8 (Public School 8) (p. 41)
reputation (p. 43)
escapade (p. 47)
quizzical (p. 49)
stoop ball (p. 53)
elaborate (p. 56)
illustrious (p. 58)
tidbit (p. 58)
sing song girl (p. 59)
grimaced (p. 60)
gossamer (p. 66)

Questions:

1. Reread page 43. Shirley says she is 10 years old. How old would you say she is? What grade should she be in?

2. Mother tells Shirley, "You are China's little ambassador." What does she mean? What are the positive and negative sides of being an ambassador?

3. Why do some of the adults in the story wink at Shirley? How does Shirley react?

4. Who is the "Hungry Ghost"?

Chapters 5-6:

Vocabulary:

regale (p. 71)
devour (p. 75)
objector (p. 79)
ritual (p. 86)
hue (p. 93)

formidable (p. 71)
quaked (p. 76)
torso (p. 80)
pauper (p. 92)
pigeon-toed (p. 89)

In the Year of the Boar and Jackie Robinson / 149

Questions:

1. Why does the Matriarch think basketball is an uncivilized game?

2. When Shirley joins the game, one of the children says, "Send her back to the laundry." What does this mean? Discuss stereotyping.

3. Read aloud from page 76, "That afternoon . . .", to the middle of page 79, "And as captain, I get first pick and Shirley's it." Discuss name-calling and ethnic identity as it relates to this passage.

4. Why do Shirley and Mabel become friends?

5. Why is Chapter 5 called "Two Black Eyes and Wispy Whiskers"?

6. Why does Mrs. Rappaport think that Jackie Robinson is an appropriate hero for the children? How does Mrs. Rappaport's speech affect Shirley?

Chapters 7-8:

Vocabulary:

mayhem (p. 98)	emanated (p. 98)
sultry (p. 99)	tyranny (p. 102)
illustrious (p. 102)	landlord (p. 106)
jaunty (p. 108)	alchemy (p. 110)
transmuted (p. 110)	ingenuity (p. 110)
adept (p. 111)	meticulous (p. 111)
tenant (p. 112)	pennant (p. 112)
gallows (p. 114)	

Questions:

1. Why do you think Shirley is infected with "Dodger fever"?

2. Why do you think Senora Rodriguez is the only character who speaks in dialect?

3. When Shirley asks her father, "Will it be difficult taking care of this house?" he says, "Probably not so difficult as raising a daughter." (p. 106) What does he mean?

Chapters 9-10:

Vocabulary:

dog days (p. 108)	molt (p. 118)
brandish/brandishing (p. 126)	oath (p. 127)

150 / In the Year of the Boar and Jackie Robinson

Questions:

1. Reread pages 120-122. How does Shirley's dream relate to her life?

Chapters 11-12:

Vocabulary:

commemorate (p. 150)
elixir (p. 151)
feigned (p. 159)
exercise in futility (p. 159)
pessimistic (p. 168)

longevity (p. 151)
filial (p. 152)
juvenile (p. 159)
campaign (p. 160)
eligible (p. 168)

Questions:

1. Reread Grandfather's story on pages 152-154. Shirley says that she wishes she were the girl in Grandfather's story. Why does Shirley want to be like the girl in the story? Do you think she is? Explain.

2. Why does Shirley encourage Emily to run for sixth-grade representative to the Christmas assembly?

3. Why does Shirley feel so ashamed when Emily says that Shirley should make the presentation to Jackie Robinson?

4. When Shirley's mother tells her that Shirley is going to have a baby brother Shirley thinks about all the things she'll do with him. "Most importantly, she would tell him about the life he would probably never know, the life she had once lived in Chungking." (p. 164) Why is this most important to her?

5. What is the impact of Jackie Robinson's school visit on Shirley's life?

6. Look at the book's illustrations. How does the artwork reflect the text? Why do you think the artist chose to illustrate those particular events in the story? Which events would you have chosen to illustrate?

RELATED BOOKS

Bales, Carol A. *Chinatown Sunday.* New York: Reilly & Lee, 1973.

Chang, Kathleen. *The Iron Moonhunter.* San Francisco: Children's Book Press, 1977.

Davidson, Margaret. *Jackie Robinson, Bravest Man in Baseball.* New York: Dell, 1988.

Handforth, Thomas. *Mei Li.* New York: Doubleday, 1938.

Hou-tien, Cheng. *The Chinese New Year.* New York: Holt, Rinehart & Winston, 1976.

Jones, Claire. *The Chinese in America.* Minneapolis, Minn.: Lerner, 1972.

Lewis, John. *The Chinese Man and the Chinese Woman.* New York: Two Continents, 1977.

_____ . *The Chinese Word for Horse.* New York: Two Continents, 1976.

_____ . *The Chinese Word for Thief.* New York: Two Continents, 1978.

Pinkwater, Manus. *Wingman.* New York: Dodd, Mead, 1975.'

Reit, Seymour, *Rice Cakes and Paper Dragons.* New York: Dodd, Mead, 1973.

Robinson, Jackie, and Alfred Duckett. *Breakthrough to the Big League.* New York: Harper, 1975.

Seeger, Elizabeth. *Eastern Religions.* New York: Crowell, 1973.

Wolff, Diane. *Chinese Writing: An Introduction.* New York: Holt, Rinehart & Winston, 1975.

Yep, Laurence. *Child of the Owl.* New York: Harper & Row, 1977.

_____ . *Dragonwings.* New York: Harper & Row, 1975.

OTHER MATERIALS

Unlearning Asian American Stereotypes: A Filmstrip and Discussion Guide. New York: Council on Interracial Books for Children, 1982.
    Available from
        Council on Interracial Books for Children
        1841 Broadway
        New York, NY 10023

ENRICHMENT ACTIVITIES

In the Year of the Boar and Jackie Robinson

1. Read books such as *Chinese Writing: An Introduction,* by Diane Wolff, or *The Chinese Word for Horse,* by John Lewis. Use large brushes and ink blocks to paint Chinese characters.

2. Research one of these topics and write a short report:
    Chinese calendar
    Chinese customs
    Chinese recipes
    Chinese New Year
    Mid-Autumn Festival

3. Select a Chinese folk tale to read. Illustrate the main events from the tale and use the pictures to help retell the tale to the group.

4. Read a biography of Jackie Robinson. Make a time line showing the major events of his life.

5. Reread Shirley's version of the Pledge of Allegiance on page 86. Compare her version to the real Pledge of Allegiance. Shirley came up with this version because she couldn't understand the words. Rewrite the Pledge of Allegiance in words that children could understand.

6. Read *Wingman* by Manus Pinkwater. Compare Donald Chen's experiences as a Chinese boy growing up in New York City to Shirley Wong's experiences. Make a chart showing how the two books are alike and different.

7. The game of mah-Jongg was invented in China. Locate a mah-Jongg set, learn how to play the game, and teach it to other members of the group.

8. In chapter 3, Shirley prays to Kwan Yin, Goddess of Mercy. Find out more about Kwan Yin. If possible, locate a picture of a statue of her. Take notes so that you can share your findings with the group.

9. Write a letter that Shirley might have written to her grandmother describing her experiences in the United States.

10. Create your own activity for *In the Year of the Boar and Jackie Robinson.*

The Indian in the Cupboard

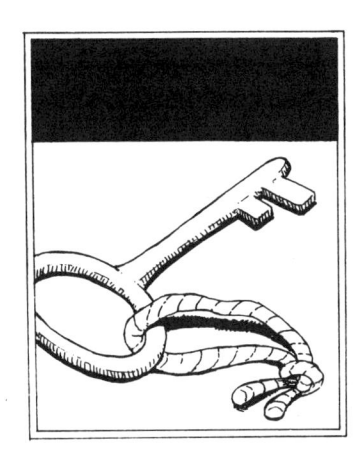

Author: Lynne Reid Banks

Illustrator: Brock Cole

Publisher, Date: Doubleday/Avon, 1980

Pages: 181

SUMMARY

For his birthday Omri receives an old metal cupboard, a mysterious gold key, and a small plastic Indian. He soon finds out that by putting the three together, he is able to make the Indian come alive. This is a fantasy adventure story that describes both the good and bad aspects of possessing something that is truly magical.

PRE-READING/MOTIVATIONAL ACTIVITIES

1. Ask the group to list things that they believe to be true about woodland Indians before the Revolutionary War. Don't edit the list at this time. The list will be used for postreading discussion.

2. Discuss different types of fantasies:

    a. Time travel—*Time at the Top* by Edward Ormondroyd
    The Time Machine by H. G. Wells

    b. High fantasy—*The Lord of the Rings* trilogy by J. R. R. Tolkien
    The Prydain Chronicles by Lloyd Alexander

    c. Humorous fantasy—The Mrs. Piggle-Wiggle series by Betty MacDonald
    The Enormous Egg by Oliver Butterworth

    d. Mystery fantasy—*The House with the Clock in Its Walls* by John Bellairs
    Elidor by Alan Garner

3. Discuss the conventions of magic found in fantasies(objects or characters with magic powers, objects or characters who grant wishes, magic wands, and so forth). Ask students to give examples of these conventions from their reading or viewing.

154 / The Indian in the Cupboard

4. Ask the students to read the title and look at the picture on the cover of the book. Ask them these questions:
   What do you think the story is going to be about?
   Who do you think the main characters are going to be?
   What do you think is the setting of the story?

VOCABULARY/DISCUSSION QUESTIONS

Chapters 1-2:

Vocabulary:

compost heap (p. 1)	biscuit tin (p. 1)
parcel (p. 2)	dustbins (p. 2)
petrified (p. 6)	minuscule (p. 11)
torso (p. 11)	buckskin (p. 11)
intricate (p. 11)	tantalizing (p. 13)
sarcastic (p. 13)	unwarily (p. 13)
miraculous (p. 14)	appalled (p. 15)
episode (p. 16)	Great White Spirit (p. 21)
longhouse (p. 21)	haughtily (p. 23)
Iroquois (p. 23)	

Questions:

1. In what country does the story take place? What evidence can you find to support your opinion?

2. Omri was "very pleased" with the cupboard even though it was used, plain, and empty. Why do you think he was pleased? (p. 3)

3. When Omri first sees the Indian alive (p. 7) he is at first frightened and then feels compelled to touch him. How does his attitude toward the Indian change by the second chapter? (p. 22) Why?

4. On page 14 Omri has discovered that the Indian is magic. "All his thoughts, all his dreams were centered on the miraculous, endless possibilities opened up by a real, live, miniature Indian of his very own." What are some of the "endless possibilities"?

5. What misconceptions did Omri have about the Indian?

6. Prediction: At the end of chapter 2 Omri feels that "nothing in his life had ever promised better." What is being promised? What do you think is going to happen next? (List predictions for later reference.)

7. List words or phrases that describe Omri in his dealings with Little Bear.

Chapters 3-7:

Vocabulary:

Algonquin (p. 27)	uncompromisingly (p. 28)
lithely (p. 28)	ransacked (p. 30)
superstitious (p. 30)	seething (p. 31)
Napoleonic Wars (p. 32)	cavalry (p. 32)
brandishing (p. 33)	platoon (p. 33)
French Foreign Legionnaires (p. 33)	Arab (p. 33)
hypnotize (p. 35)	escarpment (p. 39)
medical orderly (p. 42)	blokes (p. 42)
chap (p. 42)	trenches (p. 45)
tourniquet (p. 46)	Mohawks (p. 51)
maize (p. 51)	marrow (p. 60)
hectoring (p. 61)	privet hedge (p. 64)
pinching (stealing) (p. 67)	galvanized (p. 67)
agog (p. 68)	imperiously (p. 68)
magnanimously (p. 68)	coal scuttle (p. 71)

Questions:

1. Reread chapter 3, pages 25-27. What are the "rules" for how the magic cupboard works? How does Omri determine the rules?

2. Add to your list of words or phrases that describe Omri in his dealings with Little Bear. Talk about the changes that have occurred.

3. What is the significance of the title of chapter 6, "The Chief Is Dead, Long Live the Chief"? Why isn't the death sad?

4. How does Omri's relationship to Little Bear compare with Omri's parents' relationship to Omri?

5. Why does Omri share his secret with Patrick in chapter 7?

6. How is Patrick's reaction to Little Bear different from Omri's? Why?

7. Prediction: What do you think will happen now that Patrick knows the secret of the cupboard?

Chapters 8-12:

Vocabulary:

mulish (p. 76)	bandolier (p. 104)
raucous (p. 108)	sums (p. 115)
stealthily (p. 115)	gesticulating (p. 115)

156 / The Indian in the Cupboard

Questions:

1. Foreshadowing means giving the reader a hint about future events in the story. The author uses this technique on page 75 (beginning of chapter 8). Why do you think she uses foreshadowing here? What awful things might happen?

2. In chapter 8, Omri gives in to Patrick's demands even though it is against his better judgement. Why?

3. What do we learn about Patrick in these chapters? List words or phrases that describe him.

4. Why does Boone speak in dialect (p. 96: "Jest imagine, thankin' a piece o' yer dee-lirium tremens fer givin' you yer hat back!") when Little Bear doesn't?

5. Does Omri treat Little Bear and Boone as inferiors, equals, or superiors? Support your opinion.

6. Can you think of any new words or phrases to describe Omri? If so, add them to your list.

7. Why is Omri so upset about an adult, Mr. Johnson, knowing about Little Bear?

8. Prediction: What do you think Mr. Johnson is going to do?

Chapters 13-16:

Vocabulary:

flummoxed (p. 128)	infinitesimal (p. 134)
picture of bafflement (p. 134)	stupefaction (p. 134)
vouch (p. 138)	tea time (p. 141)
hullabaloo (p. 148)	gravitated (p. 148)
restive (p. 148)	prostrate (p. 151)
perils (p. 155)	vulnerable (p. 159)

Questions:

1. In chapters 12 and 13 (pp. 118-129) Omri and Patrick agree that the worst thing that could happen would for Little Bear and Boone to be seen by an adult. Why do they feel this way?

2. Why is Mr. Johnson so upset when he sees Little Bear?

3. What has changed Omri's dream into a nightmare? Is it Patrick, bad luck, too much responsibility, or something else? Explain.

4. All of the Indian women were made with the same mold and looked the same to Omri except for the color of their dresses. Why do you think Little Bear chooses the woman in red?

5. Why do you think the author never has the Indian woman speak?

6. Why does Little Bear's attitude toward Boone change so drastically after he shoots Boone?

7. Why did the author put Tommy into the story? Why not just have the boys take care of Little Bear and Boone when they are wounded?

8. Why does Omri give the key to his mother at the end of the story?

Questions about the book in general:

1. What kind of fantasy is this story? Explain. (*See* activity #2 in Pre-reading/Motivational Activities.)

2. What conventions of magic were used in this story? Explain. (*See* activity #3 in Pre-reading/Motivational Activities.)

3. Who do Little Bear and Boone think Omri is?

4. What is the turning point of the story?

5. How is Omri like Little Bear? How is Patrick like Boone?

6. Describe the relationship between Omri and Little Bear. How does it change throughout the story?

7. Compare the relationship of Omri and Patrick to that of Little Bear and Boone. How are these relationships alike? Different?

8. In questions 4, 5, and 6 compare and contrast story characters. One way to help students organize this kind of information is by using a Venn diagram like the one pictured below.

9. Write words or phrases that describe Patrick and Omri on the diagram. The intersection (middle) will contain words and phrases that describe both boys.

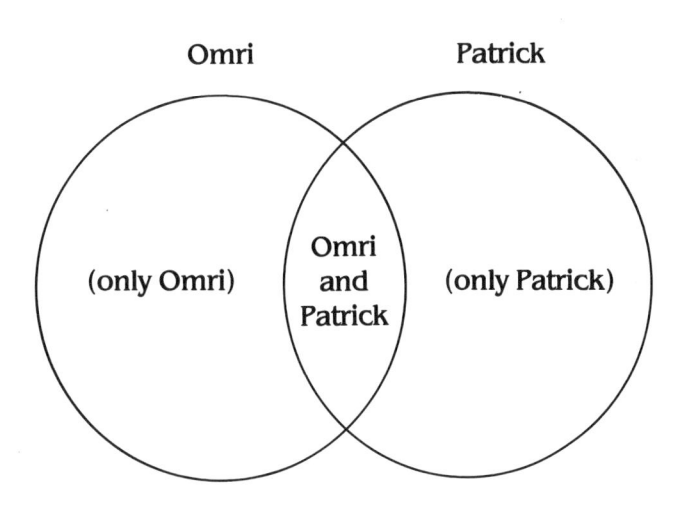

Omri   Patrick

(only Omri)   Omri and Patrick   (only Patrick)

10. Ask the students to look at the list they made of things they believed to be true about woodland Indians before the Revolutionary War. Discuss changes they would like to make after reading the story.

11. Look at the book's illustrations. How does the artwork reflect the text? Why do you think the artist chose to illustrate those particular events in the story? Which events would you have chosen to illustrate?

12. Have the group view the sound filmstrip *Unlearning "Indian" Stereotypes* (*see* Other Materials).

    Chapter 3, page 29, states, "It occurred to Omri for the first time that his idea of Indians, taken entirely from Western films, had been somehow false." At this point in the story, Omri realizes that his information about American Indians is inaccurate. Do you think the author does an adequate job of correcting the misinformation about Indians presented in the beginning chapters of the book? Why or why not?

RELATED BOOKS

Alexander, Lloyd. *The Book of Three.* New York: Holt, Rinehart & Winston, 1964.
    Other books in the Prydain Chronicles:
        The Black Cauldron, 1965.
        The Castle of Llyr, 1966.
        Taran Wanderer, 1967.
        The High King, 1968.
        The Foundling and Other Tales of Prydain, 1973

Banks, Lynne Reid. *The Fairy Rebel.* Garden City, N.Y.: Doubleday, 1988.

———. *The Farthest-Away Mountain.* Garden City, N.Y.: Doubleday, 1977.

———. *I, Houdini: The Autobiography of a Self-Educated Hamster.* Garden City, N.Y.: Doubleday, 1979.

———. *My Darling Villain.* New York: Harper & Row, 1977.

———. *The Return of the Indian.* Garden City, N.Y.: Doubleday, 1986.

———. *The Writing on the Wall.* New York: Harper & Row, 1982.

Bellairs, John. *The House with the Clock in Its Walls.* New York: Dial, 1973.

Bjorkland, Karna. *The Indians of Northeastern America.* New York: Dodd, Mead, 1969.

Butterworth, Oliver. *The Enormous Egg.* Boston: Little, Brown, 1956.

Garner, Alan. *Elidor.* New York: Henry Z. Walck, 1969.

Georgakas, Dan. *The Broken Hoop: The History of Native Americans from 1600 to 1890, from the Atlantic Coast to the Plains.* Garden City, N.Y.: Zenith/Doubleday, 1973.

Goble, Paul. *Red Hawk's Account of Custer's Last Battle: The Battle of the Little Bighorn, 25 June 1876.* New York: Pantheon, 1969.

Highwater, Jamake. *Many Smokes, Many Moons: A Chronology of American Indian History through Indian Art.* Philadelphia: Lippincott, 1978.

Hirschfelder, Arlene. *Happily May I Walk: American Indians and Alaska Natives Today.* New York: Scribner's, 1986.

Hofsinde, Robert. *Indian Picture Writing.* New York: Morrow, 1959.

Jacobson, Daniel. *Indians of North America: A Reference First Book.* New York: Watts, 1983.

LaFarge, Oliver. *The American Indian.* New York: Golden Press, 1960.

MacDonald, Betty. *Mrs. Piggle-Wiggle's Magic.* Philadelphia: Lippincott, 1949.

Ormondroyd, Edward. *Time at the Top.* Berkeley, Calif.: Parnassus Press, 1963.

Readers' Digest. *America's Fascinating Indian Heritage.* Pleasantville, N.Y.: Reader's Digest, 1978.

Ridington, Jillian, and Robin Ridington. *People of the Longhouse: How the Iroquoian Tribes Lived.* Topsfield, Mass.: Salem House, n.d.

Tolkien, J. R. R. *The Fellowship of the Ring.* Boston: Houghton Mifflin, 1956.
    Other books in The Lord of the Rings trilogy:
        The Two Towers, 1965.
        The Return of the King, 1965.

Wells, H. G. *The Time Machine.* New York: Airmont, 1964.

Wolfson, Evelyn. *From Abenaki to Zuni: A Dictionary of Native American Tribes.* New York: Walker, 1988.

OTHER MATERIALS

Unlearning "Indian" Stereotypes. Sound filmstrip. New York: Council on Interracial books for Children, 1977.
    Available from
        Council on Interracial Books for Children
        1841 Broadway
        New York, NY 10023

ENRICHMENT ACTIVITIES

The Indian in the Cupboard

1. In Little Bear's time, approximately 200 years ago, American Indian tribes varied a great deal in culture and way of life. Little Bear belonged to the Iroquois tribe, located in the northeastern United States. Find out as much as you can about the traditions, beliefs, and daily life of the Iroquois and at least one other tribe from that part of the country. Write a short report or make a set of fact cards on each tribe. Share your information with the group.

   If several people are doing this activity, make a chart like the one below, to help group members compare the tribes studied.

Tribe	Food	Shelter	Clothing	Religion	Language	Family Life

2. Little Bear was involved in the French and Indian War. Find out more about this war and share the information with the group.

3. As Little Bear mentioned in the book, the Iroquois Nation is made up of five Indian tribes. Find out more about how and why the tribal union existed. Write a short report to share this information with the group.

4. What would you do if you had the cupboard and the key? Write a short story about your adventure with the magic cupboard.

5. Where did the cupboard and the key come from? Write a story that explains how they got their powers and why they appeared at Omri's house.

6. Write a letter that Tommy, the World War I medical orderly, might have written home to his family after his encounter with Omri and Little Bear.

7. Select an episode from the story and rewrite it as a play. Choose some friends to help you read or perform the play for the group.

8. What if the key to the cupboard had not been found? Write a short story telling what happened to Little Bear and Boone.

9. What might have happened if Omri had decided not to send Little Bear, Boone, and Bright Stars back to their own times? Write a new ending for the story.

10. Make an illustrated chart or dictionary that compares British and American words for common items, for example biscuit—cookie; lorry—truck; marrow—squash.

11. Write a handbook for the care and feeding of miniatures.

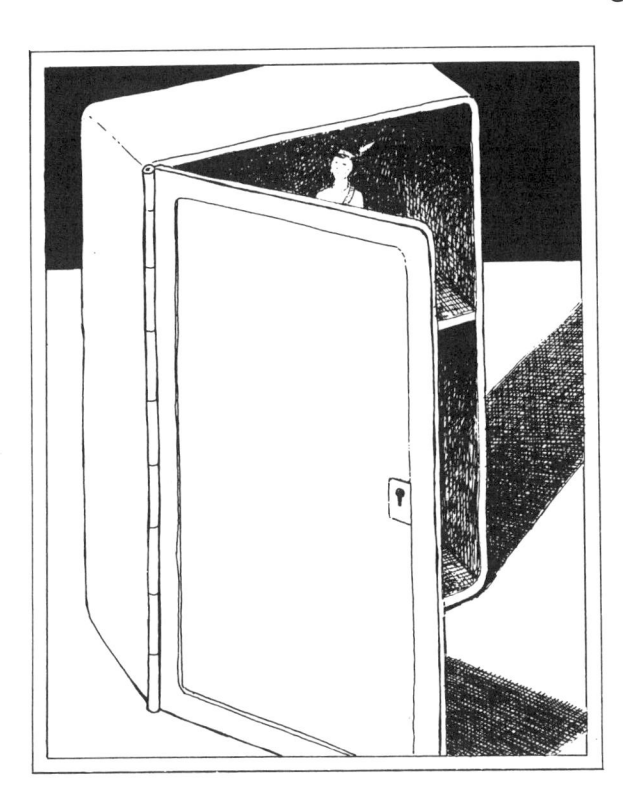

12. Make a tiny mural like the one Boone made for Omri in art class. (Adding machine tape works well for this activity.)

13. Build a home for Little Bear.

14. Read another book by Lynne Reid Banks.

15. Create your own activity for *The Indian in the Cupboard*.

Mail-Order Wings

Author: Beatrice Gormley

Illustrator: Emily Arnold McCully

Publisher, Date: E. P. Dutton/Avon, 1981

Pages: 164

SUMMARY

Andrea dreams of flying and sends for a Wonda-Wings kit from a comic book ad, even though she knows that people can't really fly under their own power. Much to her surprise the wings do work, and she is overjoyed—until she finds herself slowly becoming more birdlike. This novel is a suspenseful fantasy dealing with the pleasures and dangers of wish fulfillment.

PRE-READING/MOTIVATIONAL ACTIVITIES

1. Ask the students to read the title and look at the picture on the cover of the book. Ask them these questions:

    What do you think the story is going to be about?
    Who do you think the main character is going to be?
    What do you think is the setting of the story?

2. Rushfield, where Andrea lives, is a fictitious town located west/southwest of Boston near Route 128. Locate this area on a map of the northeastern United States. Refer back to this map to point out the location of later events in the story.

3. Show the group the advertising pages from a current comic book. Ask if anyone has ever ordered anything from this type of ad. Was what they received as wonderful as it was advertised to be?

VOCABULARY/DISCUSSION QUESTIONS

Chapters 1-3:

Vocabulary:

dormer (p. 1)
aerial (p. 6)
illusions (p. 6)
hormones (p. 14)
Latin (p. 32)
grudgingly (p. 33)
sucker (p. 37)
clambered (p. 45)

sanctuary (p. 1)
gypped (p. 6)
Rabbit (car model) (p. 9)
vireo (p. 17)
device (p. 32)
excelsior (p. 33)
inspiration (p. 38)
menacing (p. 74)

Questions:

1. What kind of person is Andrea? What kinds of things does she like? Cite examples from the story to support your opinion.

2. Why do you think Andrea is so fascinated by the "terrible" comic book? Why does she decide to keep it even though she hates it?

3. Why does she order the wings even though she thinks they will probably not work?

4. What kind of a relationship does Andrea have with her brother, Jim? Give examples of interactions between them to support your opinion.

5. Read the description of AERO-JOY JUICE on page 40. Rewrite the description in your own words. Why does Andrea decide to drink the juice even after reading the description?

6. Prediction: Now that Andrea has discovered that the wings really do work, what kinds of adventures do you think she might have?

Chapters 4-6:

Vocabulary:

Zambia (p. 53)
kimono (p. 59)
catbrier (p. 62)
sweltering (p. 69)
stanzas (p. 72)
tweed jacket (p. 87)
shinnying (p. 83)
gallivanting (p. 84)

Acapulco (p. 53)
cardamom (p. 60)
tiller (p. 64)
realtor's licence (p. 72)
Henry Wadsworth Longfellow (p. 72)
reproachfully (p. 82)
steeplejack (p. 83)

Questions:

1. Why do you think Andrea asks Jim to help her?

2. Andrea and Aunt Bets both like the poem "Excelsior." Why does each of them like it? How else are they alike? (pp. 72-73)

3. Why doesn't Andrea want anyone but Jim to know that she can fly? (p. 88)

4. Does Jim believe Andrea? (pp. 56-58, 88)

5. For Andrea being like a bird has both advantages and disadvantages. List them in two columns on a piece of paper.

6. Besides growing wings, how else is Andrea changing?

7. Prediction: What do you think will happen to her?

Chapters 7-9:

Vocabulary:

migration (p. 93)
symptoms (p. 100)
terminate (p. 103)
transition (p. 103)
unsavory (p. 105)
Mount Monadack (p. 119)
heavens to Murgatroyd (p. 121)

flyways (p. 95)
antidote (p. 103)
anxiety (p. 103)
booster dose (p. 103)
nonexistent (p. 113)
mollycoddled (p. 121)
provisions (p. 122)

Questions:

1. Add to your list of advantages and disadvantages of being a bird. At this point in the story are there more advantages or disadvantages?

2. On a map of the northeastern United States trace Andrea's route from Rushfield to the Aero-Joy Products factory in New Jersey.

3. What does Andrea think Mr. Vogel is going to do for her?

4. Why does she trust Mr. Vogel?

5. How do Jim and Aunt Bets each unknowingly encourage Andrea to fly to New Jersey?

6. Prediction: What do you think Mr. Vogel is going to do for Andrea?

Chapters 10-12:

Vocabulary:

impulsively (p. 129)
ingenious (p. 142)
fledgling (p. 143)
contemptuous (p. 146)
Icarus (p. 148)
biochemist (p. 148)
humanity (p. 155)
gingerly (p. 164)

assembly (p. 142)
sublime (p. 143)
aviatic state (p. 145)
pituitary gland (p. 146)
Leonardo da Vinci (p. 148)
perseverance (p. 150)
spurned (p. 155)

Questions:

1. List Andrea's reasons for trusting Mr. Vogel and her reasons for not trusting him. Why does she finally decide not to trust him?

2. Why does Mr. Vogel want people to turn into birds?

3. What is it about Andrea that makes her the one kid who succeeds in flying with Wonda-Wings?

4. How was turning from bird to human so much more difficult than turning from human to bird? Why?

5. Why does Jim think he's going to be in trouble when he gets home?

6. Why do you think the Coca-Cola tastes so good to Andrea?

7. How is the Mobil sign like "a banner with a strange device" saying Excelsior?

8. How does Andrea's relationship with Jim change through the course of the book?

9. Why do you think a gas station looks so beautiful to Andrea?

10. Why do you think Andrea turned into a goose rather than some other bird?

11. Look at the book's illustrations. How does the artwork reflect the text? Why do you think the artist chose to illustrate those particular events in the story? Which events would you have chosen to illustrate?

RELATED BOOKS

Burchard, Peter. *Pioneers of Flight: From Early Times to the Wright Brothers.* New York: St. Martin's Press, 1970.

Cole, Joanna. *A Bird's Body.* New York: Morrow, 1982.

Farmer, Penelope. *Summer Birds*. New York: Harcourt Brace Jovanovich, 1962.

Farmer, Penelope, and Chris Connor. *Daedalus and Icarus*. New York: Harcourt Brace Jovanovich, 1971.

Fuller, Edmund. *Henry Wadsworth Longfellow*. New York: Crowell, 1967.

Gardiner, John. *Top Secret*. Boston: Little, Brown, 1984.

Gordon, Sheila. *A Monster in the Mailbox*. New York: Random House, 1978.

Gormley, Beatrice. *Best Friend Insurance*. New York: E. P. Dutton, 1983.

_____. *Fifth Grade Magic*. New York: E. P. Dutton, 1982.

_____. *The Ghastly Glasses*. New York: E. P. Dutton, 1985.

_____. *Paul's Volcano*. Boston: Houghton Mifflin, 1987.

Kafka, Franz. *The Complete Stories and Parables*. New York: Quality Paperbacks, 1983.

Kaufmann, John. *Birds Are Flying*. New York: Crowell, 1979.

_____. *Birds in Flight*. New York: Morrow, 1970.

Langton, Jane. *The Fledgling*. New York: Harper & Row, 1980.

McDermott, Gerald. *Sun Flight*. New York: Four Winds, 1980.

Wong, Herbert H. *Ducks, Geese and Swans*. Menlo Park, Calif.: Lane Book Co., 1960.

RELATED MAGAZINES

Penny Power
   Published by Consumers Union
   P.O. Box 54861
   Boulder, CO 80322-4861

ENRICHMENT ACTIVITIES

Mail-Order Wings

1. Learn more about marketing and advertising for children. Watch television commercials aimed at children (for example, during Saturday morning cartoons). What techniques do advertisers use to get children to buy their products? You may want to look at issues of *Penny Power* magazine to get ideas (*see* Related Magazines). Report your findings to the group.

2. Read *The Fledgling* by Jane Langton. Write an essay comparing Andrea to Georgie and their flying experiences.

3. Write a story about what happened to Hubert T. Vogel after Andrea left the factory.

4. Read *Daedalus and Icarus* or *Sun Flight*. What is the moral of this myth? Compare the experiences of Icarus and Andrea.

5. Find out about bird migration. Make a poster showing the major bird migration flyways in North America.

6. Read another book by Beatrice Gormley.

7. Research early flying machines. Make illustrations of some of them and explain how they worked (or didn't work).

8. Find out how birds fly. Make illustrations that will help you explain bird flight to the group.

9. Find and read the poem "Excelsior" by H. W. Longfellow (in *Henry Wadsworth Longfellow* by Edmund Fuller). Do a reading for the group and explain its meaning.

10. Read the beginning of *Metamorphosis* by Franz Kafka. Compare Gregor Samsa's experience to that of Mr. Vogel and Andrea.

11. Write an alternate ending to the story, in which Andrea becomes a goose.

12. Write a letter that Andrea's brother, Jim, might have written to their parents describing Andrea's odd behavior.

13. Create your own activity for *Mail-Order Wings*.

On My Honor

Author: Marion Dane Bauer

Publisher, Date: Houghton Mifflin/Dell, 1986

Pages: 90

SUMMARY

Twelve-year-olds Tony and Joel have always been friends. One hot summer day they start on a bicycle trip to a state park but stop along the way for a swim in the dangerous Vermillion River. Daredevil Tony swims out too far and disappears under the surface of the water. Joel is unable to save him and now must face the task of telling their families what happened.

PRE-READING/MOTIVATIONAL ACTIVITIES

1. Ask the students to read the title and look at the picture on the cover of the book. Ask them these questions:
   What do you think the story is going to be about?
   Who do you think the main characters are going to be?
   What do you think is the setting of the story?

2. Discuss how you decide someone is going to be your friend. Who makes a better friend, someone who is just like you or who is different from you? How do you handle it when a friend asks you to do something you don't want to do or that you know you shouldn't do?

VOCABULARY/DISCUSSION QUESTIONS

Chapters 1-6:

Vocabulary:

bluffs (p. 1)	scale (climb) (p. 1)
municipal (p. 2)	hovering (p. 4)
sparse (p. 5)	surveyed (p. 6)
jaunt (p. 8)	exuberance (p. 11)
Vermillion River (p. 11)	momentum (p. 12)
Mississippi (p. 14)	elaborately (p. 15)
taunt (p. 15)	sink holes (p. 16)
currents (p. 16)	whirlpools (p. 16)
sewage (p. 18)	gawk (p. 19)

(vocabulary continues on next page)

chlorine (p. 20)
realigned (p. 25)
angle (p. 28)
deceptively (p. 31)
skulked (p. 34)

mimicked (p. 21)
agitated (p. 26)
paddle wheeler (p. 28)
barrage (p. 31)

Questions:

1. What is Tony like? What is Joel like? What kind of a relationship do they have?

2. How are the boys like the bikes they own? (pp. 10-11)

3. Joel asks his father for permission to do something he really doesn't want to do. Why? (pp. 4-9)

4. Why do you think Tony decides he'd rather go swimming than climb the bluffs? (pp. 14-16)

5. Both boys have much to fear. What is Joel afraid of? What is Tony afraid of?

6. List the ways the boys differ from each other. Try to think of reasons for these differences.

7. Why does Joel think the police are going to "get him"?

8. Why does Joel believe that Tony's drowning is his fault?

9. Prediction: What do you think Joel will do?

Chapters 7-12:

Vocabulary:

nonchalance (p. 47)
giddily (p. 54)
circulars (p. 63)
fretting (p. 66)
silhouetted (p. 77)
accusation (p. 86)

semi (truck) (p. 48)
amended (p. 61)
reverently (p. 65)
skeptical (p. 67)
simultaneously (p. 78)
pummel (p. 87)

Questions:

1. Why does Joel head for the park instead of going right home? (p. 48)

2. Reread pages 49-50. Why does Joel make up this elaborate story about leaving Tony at the river?

3. "He spoke out of the deep calm that had taken hold of him sometime in the long afternoon." Why do you think Joel feels calm at this point in the story? (p. 55)

4. Why do you think Joel is so angry with his parents? (chap. 8)

5. Why does Joel treat Bobby so erratically while they are on the paper route? (chap. 9)

6. Why do you think Joel can't wash away the smell of the river?

7. What does Joel really want from his father?

8. Why does Joel's father apologize to him? (pp. 84-85)

9. What makes Joel finally begin to cry? (p. 88)

10. What is honor? Is Joel honorable?

RELATED BOOKS

Bauer, Marion Dane. *Foster Child*. New York: Seabury, 1977.

_____ . *Like Mother, Like Daughter*. New York: Ticknor & Fields, 1985.

_____ . *Rain of Fire*. Boston: Houghton Mifflin, 1983.

_____ . *Shelter from the Wind*. New York: Seabury, 1976.

_____ . *Tangled Butterfly*. Boston: Houghton Mifflin, 1980.

_____ . *Touch the Moon*. New York: Ticknor & Fields, 1987.

Bramwell, Marlyn. *Rivers and Lakes*. New York: Watts, 1986.

Cohn, Janice. *I Had a Friend Named Peter*. New York: Morrow, 1987.

Fassler, Joan. *My Grandpa Died Today*. New York: Human Science Press, 1983.

Naden, Corinne. *The First Book of Rivers*. New York: Watts, 1967.

Paterson, Katherine. *Bridge to Terabithia*. New York: Harper & Row, 1977.

Richter, Elizabeth, *Losing Someone You Love: When a Brother or Sister Dies*. New York: Putnam, 1986.

Simon, Norma. *The Saddest Time*. Chicago: Whitman, 1986.

_____ . *We Remember Philip*. Chicago: Whitman, 1979.

Smith, Doris Buchanan. *A Taste of Blackberries*. New York: Crowell, 1973.

ENRICHMENT ACTIVITIES

On My Honor

1. Read another book by Marion Dane Bauer. Write an essay comparing the characters in the book you read with those in *On My Honor*.

2. Read *A Taste of Blackberries*. Write an essay comparing the two books, keeping in mind that *A Taste of Blackberries* is written for younger readers.

3. What makes many rivers dangerous places to swim? Do some research on the subject, take notes, and report your findings to the group.

4. Make a map showing the route from the boys' houses to Starved Rock. Be sure to include the river and the bridge, as well as a key to the symbols you use and a mileage scale.

5. Write a letter that Joel might have written to Tony's parents in the days following Tony's death.

6. What is honor? Write an essay.

7. Read a book or article about how people deal with the death of a friend or a family member. Share what you learn with the group. As a group decide whether Joel's reaction to Tony's death was typical or unusual.

8. Interview several people to find out how and when they learned to swim. Report your findings to the group.

9. Survey 50 or more people to find out how many of them know how to swim. Ask the people who do not know how to swim why they have never learned. Report your results to the group.

10. Create your own activity for *On My Honor*.

GRADE SIX

Dragonwings

Author: Laurence Yep

Publisher, Date: Harper & Row, 1975

Pages: 248

SUMMARY

It is 1903 and Moon Shadow, a young Chinese boy, has just arrived in San Francisco to join his father, Windrider, and work with him in a Chinatown laundry. Windrider dreams of building a flying machine, and he succeeds in spite of the San Francisco earthquake, limited income, and everpresent racial discrimination.

PRE-READING/MOTIVATIONAL ACTIVITIES

1. Ask the students to read the title and look at the picture on the cover of the book. Ask them these questions:
   What do you think the story is going to be about?
   Who do you think the main characters are going to be?
   What do you think is the setting of the story?

2. Find the Middle Kingdom (an archaic name for China); Canton, China; California; and San Francisco on a world map. Discuss how people traveled from China to San Francisco in 1903.

3. Provide students with background information about early Chinese immigration to this country using books such as *Passage to the Golden Gate: A History of the Chinese in America to 1910* and *An Illustrated History of the Chinese in America* (see Related Books).

4. Point out that the author tries to convey the feeling that the story is told in Chinese by always using italics to indicate English terms or words spoken in English.

VOCABULARY/DISCUSSION QUESTIONS

Chapters 1-3:

Vocabulary:

Land of the Golden Mountains (p. 1)	Middle Kingdom (p. 1)
white demons (p. 1)	lynched (p. 1)
paddies (p. 2)	clans (p. 2)
people of the Tang (p. 3)	dynasty (p. 3)
heirlooms (p. 4)	Jade Emperor (p. 5)
tuberculosis (p. 7)	dowries (p. 8)
the Company (p. 9)	Canton (p. 10)
bilge (p. 12)	kinsmen (p. 12)
immigrants (p. 12)	flatiron (p. 15)
tunic (p. 16)	brothels (p. 18)
amiably (p. 19)	moon guitar (p. 19)
vendors (p. 19)	prostitutes (p. 21)
prosperity (p. 21)	superior man (p. 21)
Confucius (p. 21)	conventional (p. 23)
pious (p. 23)	Mah-Jongg (p. 23)
devout (p. 23)	Buddhist (p. 23)
dialect (p. 24)	Boxer Rebellion (p. 25)
socialist (p. 25)	provincial (p. 25)
attired (p. 26)	raiment (p. 27)
Manchu (p. 27)	queues (p. 27)
drudgelike (p. 28)	opium (p. 29)
insolent (p. 29)	crystal set (p. 32)
filaments (p. 33)	sinew (p. 40)
iridescently (p. 42)	aerial (p. 43)
unalloyed (p. 45)	malleable (p. 45)
knickknack (P. 47)	meticulous (p. 47)
rheumatic (p. 47)	

Questions:

1. Why does Moon Shadow decide to go to the Golden Mountain?

2. Read aloud from the bottom of page 18 ("Suddenly I felt as if I had come home") to the bottom of page 21. Discuss why the town of the Tang people seemed like such a good place to Moon Shadow.

3. What does Moon Shadow learn about the "demons" during his first day in the city? (chaps. 1-2)

4. Why does Moon Shadow believe Father's dragon story?

5. What do we learn about Father in the first three chapters?

6. How does hearing the dragon story change Moon Shadow and Father's relationship? Why?

Chapters 4-6

Vocabulary:

hunkered down (p. 52)	clutch (car) (p. 58)
surly (p. 59)	begrudge (p. 59)
contraption (p. 61)	brotherhood (p. 68)
Sleepers (p. 68)	fox (slang) (p. 73)
abacus (p. 76)	simpering (p. 81)
mealy-mouthed (p. 81)	pain-goaded (p. 81)
tainted (p. 83)	wizened (p. 87)
prudent (p. 94)	celluloid collar (p. 96)
heathen (p. 102)	gingham (p. 105)
stereopticon (p. 106)	magic lantern (p. 107)
antiquated (p. 109)	repertory (p. 109)

Questions:

1. In chapter 4, page 50, Moon Shadow says, "I worked sixteen hours a day and had never been happier in my life." Why do you think he is happy when he must work so hard?

2. In Moon Shadow's first months in San Francisco, what do he and his father learn about being a father and a son?

3. Why is chapter 4 called "Tests"?

4. Discuss what the reader learns about the Sleepers in chapters 4 and 5, pages 68-90.

5. Contrast Moon Shadow and Black Dog's views of their lives in San Francisco.

6. Why do you think Father feels that he can follow the dragon's ways better among the demons than among the Tang people? (pp. 91-92)

7. Why does Father shake hands with Uncle instead of bowing? (p. 94)

8. What more do we learn about Father in chapters 4-6?

9. How is Miss Whitlaw different from other demons? How is she like other demons?

176 / Dragonwings

Chapters 7-9:

Vocabulary:

lair (p. 114)
laying siege (p. 121)
erratically (p. 124)
out-ornery (p. 126)
awash with gore (p. 128)
curvature (p. 129)
correspondence (p. 134)
realign (p. 147)
pagan (p. 149)
boycott (p. 151)
querulous (p. 157)
fundament (p. 161)

jasmine (p. 115)
schematics (p. 123)
wing configuration (p. 124)
whoppers (p. 126)
junk (p. 129)
exploits (p. 130)
taut (p. 138)
monopolize (p. 149)
somber (p. 150)
boisterous (p. 156)
candelabrum (p. 159)
shanghaier (p. 161)

Questions:

1. Why is chapter 7 called "Educations"?

2. What does Miss Whitlaw mean in her statement at the bottom of page 32? Do you agree with Moon Shadow that Miss Whitlaw is a wise woman?

3. Why does Father put a red ribbon in his queue on the day of their first picnic?

4. Why do Father and Uncle reconcile during The Feast of Pure Brightness? (chap. 9)

5. How do different people react to the earthquake? Why do you think they react in these ways?

6. Prediction: What do you think will happen to Miss Whitlaw and Robin? To Moon Shadow and Father?

Chapters 10-12:

Vocabulary:

sprightlier (p. 182)
sardonically (p. 195)
plateau (p. 201)
struts (p. 211)
elevators (p. 212)
warping mechanism (p. 213)
shrewd (p. 217)
cordial (p. 235)

ineptitude (p. 185)
scandalized (p. 199)
wharves (p. 209)
horizontal rudders (p. 212)
banking (p. 212)
cradle (p. 213)
whelped (p. 228)
cantankerous (p. 243)

Questions:

1. Why do you think Uncle tells the Company to use the millionaire's purple sheets for the tent?

2. Why do Moon Shadow and Father move to Oakland?

3. How is it easier for Father to fly than for Mother to live in the village? (p. 204)

4. Why doesn't Mother want Moon Shadow to show Father her letter? (pp. 206-207)

5. When it is obvious that Father is going to need help if he is to fly, why doesn't he ask Uncle or Miss Whitlaw for help? (pp. 220-224)

6. Why do you think Father decides not to build another Dragonwings?

7. Where does the climax of this story occur? Explain your answer.

8. What are the qualities of a superior man or woman? (pp. 21, 174, 200)

9. View and discuss the filmstrip *Unlearning Asian American Stereotypes* (see Other Materials).

RELATED BOOKS

Bales, Carol A. *Chinatown Sunday*. New York: Reilly & Lee, 1973.

Baskin, Hosie. *Book of Dragons*. New York: Knopf, 1985.

Blumberg, Rhoda. *The Truth about Dragons*. New York: Four Winds, 1980.

Brennan, Dennis. *Adventures in Courage: The Skymasters*. Chicago: Reilly & Lee, 1968.

Brown, Billye Walker, and Walter R. Brown. *Historical Catastrophes: Earthquakes*. Reading, Mass.: Addisonian Press, 1974.

Chang, Kathleen. *The Iron Moonhunter*. Chicago: Children's Book Press, 1977.

Chu, Daniel and Samuel Chu. *Passage to the Golden Gate: A History of the Chinese in America to 1910*. Garden City, N.Y.: Zenith/Doubleday, 1967.

Coatsworth, Elizabeth. *The Cat Who Went to Heaven*. New York: Macmillan, 1930.

Fleming, Thomas J. *The Golden Door: The Story of American Immigration*. New York: Grosset & Dunlap, 1970.

Gilfond, Henry. *Disastrous Earthquakes*. New York: Watts, 1981.

Glines, Carroll V. *The Wright Brothers: Pioneers of Power Flight*. New York: Watts, 1968.

Greenleaf, Barbara Kaye. *American Fever: The Story of American Immigration.* New York: Four Winds, 1970.

Johnson Enid. *Rails across the Continent: The Story of the First Transcontinental Railroad.* New York: Julian Messner, 1965.

Jones, Claire. *The Chinese in America.* Minneapolis, Minn.: Lerner, 1972.

McCunn, Ruthanne Lum. *An Illustrated History of the Chinese in America.* San Francisco: Design Enterprises of San Francisco, 1979.

———. *Pie-biter.* San Francisco: Design Enterprises of San Francisco, 1983.

Manning-Saunders, Ruth. *The Book of Dragons.* New York: E. P. Dutton, 1964.

Miller, Marilyn. *The Transcontinental Railroad.* Morristown, N.J.: Silver Burdett, 1986.

Nixon, Hershell H., and Joan Lowery Nixon. *Earthquakes: Nature in Motion.* New York: Dodd, Mead, 1981.

Norton, Andre. *Dragon Magic.* New York: Crowell, 1972.

Pinkwater, Manus. *Wingman.* New York: Dodd, Mead, 1975.

Reit, Seymour. *Rice Cakes and Paper Dragons.* New York: Dodd, Mead, 1973.

Seeger, Elizabeth, *Eastern Religions.* New York: Crowell, 1973.

Shippen, Katherine B. *A Bridle for Pegasus.* New York: Viking, 1951.

Smith, Norman F. *Wings of Feathers, Wings of Flame: The Science and Technology of Aviation.* Boston: Little, Brown, 1972.

Stein, Conrad. *The Story of the Flight at Kitty Hawk.* Chicago: Children's Press, 1981.

Sung, Betty Lee. *An Album of Chinese Americans.* New York: Watts, 1977.

Urquhart, David Inglis. *The Airplane and How It Works.* New York: Henry Z. Walck, 1973.

Wellman, Paul I. *Race to the Golden Spike.* Boston: Houghton Mifflin, 1961.

Wolff, Diane. *Chinese Writing: An Introduction.* New York: Holt, Rinehart & Winston, 1975.

Yep, Laurence. *Child of the Owl.* New York: Harper & Row, 1977.

———. *Dragon of the Lost Sea.* New York: Harper & Row, 1982.

_____. *Dragon Steel*. New York: Harper & Row, 1985.

_____. *Kind Hearts and Gentle Monsters*. New York: Harper & Row, 1982.

_____. *The Mark Twain Murders*. New York: Four Winds, 1982.

_____. *Mountain Light*. New York: Harper & Row, 1985.

_____. *Sea Glass*. New York: Harper & Row, 1979.

_____. *The Serpent's Child*. New York: Harper & Row, 1984.

_____. *Sweetwater*. New York: Harper & Row, 1973.

Yolen, Jane. *World on a String: The Story of Kites*. Cleveland: World Publishing Co., 1968.

Zisfein, Melvin B. *Flight: A Panorama of Aviation*. New York: Pantheon/Random House, 1981.

OTHER MATERIALS

Unlearning Asian American Stereotypes: A Filmstrip and Discussion Guide. New York: Council on Interracial Books for Children, 1982.
    Available from
    Council on Interracial Books for Children
    1841 Broadway
    New York, NY 10023

ENRICHMENT ACTIVITIES

Dragonwings

1. Do a time line for flight from hot air balloons to the space shuttle.

2. Research the San Francisco earthquake of 1906. Write a newspaper account of the earthquake using the information you find plus what you learned from *Dragonwings*. Be sure to include a headline. You may want to create an entire front page with related articles of earthquake news.

3. Write an illustrated report that shows and explains why earthquakes occur. Be sure to include information about the San Andreas Fault.

4. Dragons are part of the folklore of many different cultures. Research dragons from at least three parts of the world. Make a drawing of each dragon and list its attributes (appearance, powers, origin, temperament, and so forth).

5. Read *Dragon Magic* by Andre Norton. Give a book talk to the group.

6. Research the role of the Chinese in building American railroads. *The Iron Moonhunter* by Kathleen Chang and *Pie-biter* by Ruthanne Lum McCunn are fictionalized but accurate accounts of this period in Chinese-American history. Write a short story about a day in the life of a Chinese railroad worker.

7. Windrider is known for the beautiful kites that he builds. Construct a kite (*see* Related Books).

8. Windrider had to do a great deal of research in order to construct an airplane that would fly. Find out more about aerodynamics. Give a report on how airplanes fly.

9. Reread the dragon story in chapter 3, pages 35-46. Draw or paint a picture of the dragon or make a comic strip that tells the dragon story.

10. In chapter 3, pages 31-32, Moon Shadow describes the naming custom of the Tang people. If you could choose names for yourself, what name would you pick for yourself as a baby? Before you started school? Now? When you are grown? Write an essay explaining the reasons for your choices.

11. If you were to come back in your next life as an animal, what animal would you like to be and why? Draw a picture of the animal and explain to the group the reasons for your choice.

12. Read another book by Laurence Yep.

13. Find out more about the Eastern religious belief in reincarnation. *The Cat Who Went to Heaven*, by Elizabeth Coatsworth, is an interesting fictional account of reincarnation in the Buddhist tradition.

14. Write a letter Moon Shadow might have written to his mother about the day of Dragonwings' flight.

15. Write a report on Chinese immigration. What is unique about the Chinese immigration experience in the United States prior to World War II? How did it differ from the experiences of other ethnic groups? How did the immigration laws of that time affect the Chinese?

16. Create your own activity for *Dragonwings*.

The Hero and the Crown

Author: Robin McKinley

Publisher, Date: Greenwillow/Ace, 1984

Pages: 227

SUMMARY

The people of Damar are afraid of the king's daughter, Aerin, because they believe she may have inherited her mother's witch powers. Aerin is determined to prove herself to them by becoming a dragonslayer. Her success in this role leads her to a confrontation with a giant dragon and a quest for the Hero's Crown which will restore peace to the kingdom of Damar. This fantasy novel won the 1985 Newbery Medal.

PRE-READING/MOTIVATIONAL ACTIVITIES

1. This book is an example of high fantasy. It is set entirely in an imaginary place and deals with the battle between good and evil. J. R. R. Tolkien's The Lord of the Rings trilogy is another example of high fantasy. Ask the group to brainstorm a list of people, objects, and events that might occur in such a story. Ask if anyone can think of other examples of high fantasy.

2. Discuss vocabulary pertaining to horses and horseback riding: livery, girth, pommel, bit, paddock, equerry, croup, withers, cantle, and forelock.

3. Ask the students to read the title and look at the picture on the cover of the book. Ask them these questions:
    What do you think the story is going to be about?
    Who do you think the main characters are going to be?
    Who is the Hero?
    What is the Crown?

VOCABULARY/DISCUSSION QUESTIONS

Chapters 1-5:

Damarian Vocabulary:

   Damar: country where the story takes place (p. 4)
   sola: rank of royalty (p. 4)
   hafor: servants of the household (p. 5)

Aerinha: goddess of honor and of flame (p. 17)
surka: sacred plant of royalty (p. 19)
mik-bar: a food considered a treat (p. 18)
kenet: ointment that protects against fire (p. 31)
redroot (astzoran): low, weedy plant that grows in meadows; key ingredient in kenet (p. 31)
malak: a drink
saha: type of fruit used for jam (p. 73)
kelar: the gift of supernatural powers (p. 148)
foltza: wildcats (p. 160)
yerig: wild dog (p. 162)

Chapter 1:

Vocabulary:

brood (p. 3)
deference (p. 4)
mesmerizing (p. 7)
entourage (p. 8)
gainsay (p. 9)

preoccupied (p. 3)
hoyden (p. 4)
livery (p. 8)
dereliction (p. 8)

Questions:

1. Foreshadowing means giving the reader a hint about future events in the story. In chapter 1, what do you think the author is foreshadowing for Aerin? For other characters? For Damar?

Chapters 2-4:

Vocabulary:

haggard (p. 14)
scabbard (p. 16)
posset (p. 18)
throwback (p. 22)
paddock (p. 28)
vermin (p. 27)
armament (p. 30)
insinuated (p. 32)

basilisk (p. 14)
scuttling (p. 17)
minions (p. 19)
translucent (p. 24)
unwary (p. 27)
scurrilous (p. 30)
uniquely (p. 31)

Questions:

1. Damar is a fictitious country, existing in an undefined time period. What have we learned so far about Damar's landscape, royal family, customs, and government? What other information has the author given us about Damar?

2. After Aerin ate the surka leaves, she almost died. How did this experience contribute to her taming of Talat and discovering the book containing the kenet recipe?

3. The last line of chapter 4 says, "It was that day that a small but terrible hope first bloomed in Aerin's heart." How can hope be terrible? What do you think Aerin's hope was?

Chapters 5-9:

Vocabulary:

coyly (p. 35)	dragooned (p. 36)
sovereigns (p. 37)	predecessor (p. 38)
genocidal (p. 37)	wheedled (p. 40)
hiatus/hiatuses (p. 41)	officiated (p. 43)
marauding (p. 44)	exconvalescent (p. 44)
transcendent (p. 46)	liaison (p. 48)
unique (p. 50)	termagant (p. 51)
lackey (p. 57)	deft (p. 57)
pomander (p. 58)	apothecary (p. 58)
adornment (p. 59)	academic (p. 59)
entail (p. 59)	atrocity (p. 61)
wistfully (p. 61)	flinching (p. 61)
intransigence (p. 65)	skirmishes (p. 65)
succinctly (p. 66)	immoderate (p. 67)
warding (p. 68)	mage (p. 69)
meticulousness (p. 71)	epithets (p. 71)
treacherous (p. 71)	chastened (p. 71)
rehabilitated (p. 72)	tactical (p. 73)
strategic (p. 73)	nonchalantly (p. 75)
sidled (p. 75)	

Questions:

1. Why don't Aerin and Tor talk about her reason for wanting to learn swordcraft? (chap. 5, p. 42)

2. How does Aerin's eighteenth birthday mark a turning point in her life?

3. Why does magic have such a strong negative effect on Aerin?

4. In chapter 8, the Hero's Crown is first introduced. What do we find out about the Hero's Crown?

5. Reread the scene involving Aerin and Arlbeth on pages 73-74. What do we learn about their relationship in this scene?

6. Prediction: At the end of chapter 9, Aerin has mastered Talat, the sword, and the kenet. What do you think she is going to do next?

Chapters 10-11:

Vocabulary:

protocol (p. 79)
lair (p. 79)
bystander (p. 81)
antechamber (p. 88)
beseeching (p. 91)
poultice (p. 96)

petitioner (p. 79)
noncombatant (p. 81)
hummock (p. 82)
emissary (p. 89)
rhetorical (p. 91)
defter (p. 96)

Questions:

1. When Aerin leaves the city to kill her first dragon, she gets away unnoticed. "Her luck—or something—was good." (p. 80) What might that "something" have been?

2. What do we learn about dragons in chapter 10?

3. Does Gebeth think that Aerin's killing the dragon is a good thing or a bad thing? (p. 87) Explain.

4. Does Arlbeth think that Aerin's killing the dragon is a good thing or a bad thing? Explain.

5. Why does Aerin want to kill dragons?

6. Prediction: Reread the last paragraph on page 98. Do you think Arlbeth will let Aerin ride with him? Give reasons to support your prediction.

Chapters 12-16:

Vocabulary:

alcove (p. 101)
equerry (p. 102)
wind-broken (p. 103)
contingency (p. 105)
gout (of fire) (p. 108)
galls (p. 112)
ebbed (p. 114)
craven (p. 125)
wraith (p. 135)
withers (p. 137)

courtiers (p. 101)
crucially (p. 103)
acrid (p. 104)
gauntlets (p. 106)
ravaged (p. 111)
girth (p. 113)
impulsion (p. 118)
auditors (p. 126)
insidious (p. 137)

186 / The Hero and the Crown

Questions:

1. Why did Aerin go out to kill Maur?

2. Why do you think the kenet doesn't work against Maur? (p. 108)

3. After Talet goes down, Aerin runs forward even though she thinks it is too late. (p. 109) Why does she think it is too late?

4. Why does Aerin succeed in killing Maur? Is it luck, skill, or something else?

5. After she killed Maur, Aerin picked up the red dragon stone from the ashes. Do you think this stone will bring her good or evil? Why?

6. On her way back to the City, Aerin feels "dread for what was to come." (p. 121) What is she dreading?

7. What does Aerin's newly straightened hair signify? (p. 124)

8. After Maur's head is hung on the wall of the castle he says, "I am the shape of their fear." What does this mean?

9. After seeing Maur's skull, Aerin hears voices. (pp. 127-128) Are people really saying these things about her or are the voices fantasies brought to life by Maur?

10. Why doesn't Luthe come to the City to get Aerin?

11. What is Luthe trying to prepare Aerin for? (p. 142)

Chapters 17-20:

Vocabulary:

tracery (p. 143)
self-aggrandizement (p. 144)
shunting (p. 149)
juggernaut (p. 156)
aught (p. 164)
vortex (p. 171)
mundane (p.178)

bole (p. 143)
purblind (p. 145)
morganatic (p. 149)
sojourn (p. 157)
usurp (p. 162)
fluctuations (p. 168)
inglorious (p. 172)

The Hero and the Crown / 187

Questions:

1. Reread page 145 from "The stronger the Gift . . ." on. When Luthe says, "I'm not entirely human myself," what does he mean?

2. On page 146 Luthe says, "If it's any comfort, I'm not quite mortal either." What does he mean by that?

3. On page 147 Luthe says, "I followed you, you know, when you went under. I-I had to make a rather bad bargain to bring you back again. It was not a bargain I was expecting to have to make." What bargain do you think he had to make?

4. On page 148 Luthe tells Aerin that she and demonkind are related. How can Aerin, the hero of the story, be related to demons?

5. As Aerin's health returns she reflects that immortality was a terrible price to pay for being alive. (p. 149) How can this be so?

6. Reread the paragraph that begins at the bottom of page 152. What does Aerin mean when she says that "Maur *had* killed her"?

7. Why does Luthe prefer Aerin to her mother?

8. On their journey toward the tower Aerin says, "We are no longer in Damar." How does she know that?

9. On the journey toward the tower Aerin begins to hear "little gibbering voices." Do you think they are coming from inside or outside of her head?

10. Aerin's first attempt to enter Agsded's tower fails, but when the animals charge the tower, they are successful in breaking into it. Why do you think the animals succeed when she does not?

11. Do a choral reading of the four paragraphs beginning on page 170 with "By the wings. . . ." Discuss how the author uses rhythm and language to describe the scene more vividly.

12. Once Aerin and Agsded are face to face, how does he seek to defeat her? List the ways.

13. In the middle of her combat with Agsded Aerin says, "I must learn to go forward of my own free will." Whose will has it been until this point in the story?

14. The surka wreath kills Agsded when the sword does not. After Agsded dies all the surka disappears. How do you explain this?

15. Why do you think Aerin is chosen as the one to defeat Agsded and find the Hero's Crown?

188 / The Hero and the Crown

Chapters 21-25:

Vocabulary:

>   chop logic (p. 194)
>   forbearance (p. 196)
>   surcease (p. 204)
>   keening (p. 209)
>   precluded (p. 211)
>   miasma (p. 212)
>   asperity (p. 216)
>   stringent (p. 221)
>   antipathy (p. 223)
>   uncanny (p. 226)

>   premises (p. 194)
>   swathe (p. 203)
>   monoliths (p. 206)
>   sibilant (p. 209)
>   ascendance (p. 211)
>   lethargy (p. 211)
>   beleaguered (p. 220)
>   hidebound (p. 222)
>   refurbish (p. 224)

Questions:

1. Which is more powerful, the dragon's bloodstone or the Hero's Crown? Why?

2. Why doesn't Aerin ask Luthe about his origins on their last day together? (p. 192)

3. Are the soldiers from the North demons?

4. Why would keeping Maur's head have such a bad effect on the kingdom?

5. Why does Aerin laugh at the end of chapter 23?

6. Why does Aerin say yes to Tor's proposal so easily?

7. Why does Aerin seem ambivalent about Arlbeth's death? (p. 220) Could she have saved him? Explain.

8. Why do you think the final battle with the Northerners came to be called Maur's Battle?

9. Prediction: Do you think Aerin finds Luthe again? Why or why not?

10. Compile a list of examples of the Gift's powers (mends plates, starts fire, and so forth). Describe the Gift.

RELATED BOOKS

Alexander Lloyd. *The Book of Three.* New York: Holt, Rinehart & Winston, 1964.
    Other books in The Prydain Chronicles:
        The Black Cauldron, 1965.
        The Castle of Llyr, 1966.
        Taran Wanderer, 1967.
        The High King, 1968.
        The Foundling and Other Tales of Prydain, 1973.

Alexander Lloyd. *Westmark.* New York: E. P. Dutton, 1981.
    Other books in the Westmark Trilogy:
        The Kestrel, 1982.
        The Beggar Queen, 1984.

Anderson, C. W. *C. W. Anderson's Complete Book of Horses and Horsemanship.* New York: Macmillan, 1963.

Baskin, Hosie. *Book of Dragons.* New York: Knopf, 1985.

Blumberg, Rhoda. *The Truth about Dragons.* New York: Four Winds, 1980.

Fonstad, Karen Wynn. *The Atlas of Pern.* New York: Ballantine, 1984.

LeGuin, Ursula K. *A Wizard of Earthsea.* New York: Atheneum, 1968.
    Other books in the Earthsea Trilogy:
        The Tombs of Atuan, 1971.
        The Farthest Shore, 1972.

McCaffrey, Anne. *Dragonflight.* New York: Ballantine, 1975.
    Other books in the Dragonriders of Pern series:
        Dragonquest, 1979.
        The White Dragon, 1980.
    Other books set on Pern:
        Dragonsong, 1976.
        Dragonsinger, 1977.
        Dragondrums, 1979.
        Moreta, Dragonlady of Pern, 1983.
        Dragonsdawn, 1988.
        Renegades of Pern, 1989.

McKinley, Robin. *Beauty: A Retelling of the Story of Beauty and the Beast.* New York: Harper & Row, 1978.

_____. *The Blue Sword.* New York: Greenwillow, 1982.

_____. *The Door in the Hedge.* New York: Greenwillow, 1981.

——— . *Imaginary Lands.* New York: Greenwillow, 1985.

Manning-Saunders, Ruth. *The Book of Dragons.* New York: E. P. Dutton, 1964.

Minard, Rosemary. *Womanfolk and Fairytales.* Boston: Houghton Mifflin, 1975.

Norton, Andre. *The Crystal Gryphon.* New York: Atheneum, 1972.

——— . *Dragon Magic.* New York: Crowell, 1972.

——— . *Gryphon in Glory.* New York: Atheneum, 1981.

——— . *No Night without Stars.* New York: Atheneum, 1975.

——— . *Witchworld.* New York: Ace, 1963.
  Other Witch World books:
    Web of the Witch World, 1964.
    Three against the Witch World, 1965.
    Warlock of the Witch World, 1967.
    Sorceress of the Witch World, 1968.

Pervier, Evelyn. *Horsemanship: Basics for Beginners.* New York: Julian Messner, 1984.

Phelps, Ethel Johnston. *Tatterhood and Other Tales.* Old Westbury, N.Y.: Feminist Press, 1978.

Riordan, James. *The Woman in the Moon and Other Tales of Forgotten Heroines.* New York: Dial, 1985.

Tolkien, J. R. R. *The Fellowship of the Ring.* Boston: Houghton Mifflin, 1965.
  Other books in The Lord of the Rings trilogy:
    The Two Towers, 1965.
    The Return of the King, 1965.

Tolkien, J. R. R. *The Hobbit.* Prequel to The Lord of the Rings. Boston: Houghton Mifflin, 1937.

ENRICHMENT ACTIVITIES

The Hero and the Crown

1. Make a Damarian dictionary. Use the words in the story and make up more Damarian words of your own.

2. Write a recipe for kenet.

3. Draw a cartoon strip of Aerin's battle with Maur. Reread the description on pages 107-110.

4. Damar has its own mythology and gods (for example, God That Isn't There (p. 169), Seven Perfect Gods (pp. 149-150), and mother of all horses (p. 170)). Make up a Damarian myth using what you have learned about Damarian mythology from *The Hero and the Crown*.

5. Make a map of Damar.

6. Do a report on dragons. Include information about dragons from different cultures.

7. Luthe doesn't tell Aerin where the sword, Gontieran, came from and how it came into his possession. Write a story explaining these things.

8. On page 181 the author foreshadows events that will happen far in Damar's future, as told in *The Blue Sword*. Read this sequel to *The Hero and the Crown*.

9. This is an unusual fantasy in that the main character is female. Read another fantasy with a strong female character, such as McCaffrey's Dragonriders of Pern series, Phelps's *Tatterhood and Other Tales*, and Riordan's *The Woman in the Moon and Other Tales of Forgotten Heroines*.

10. Draw pictures of the main characters and/or key events in the story.

11. What would you do if you had the Gift? Write a story showing its good and bad effects.

12. Read another fantasy that is set entirely in an imaginary place. Authors of such books include Lloyd Alexander, Ursula LeGuin, Andre Norton, Anne McCaffrey, and J. R. R. Tolkien.

13. Create your own activity for *The Hero and the Crown*.

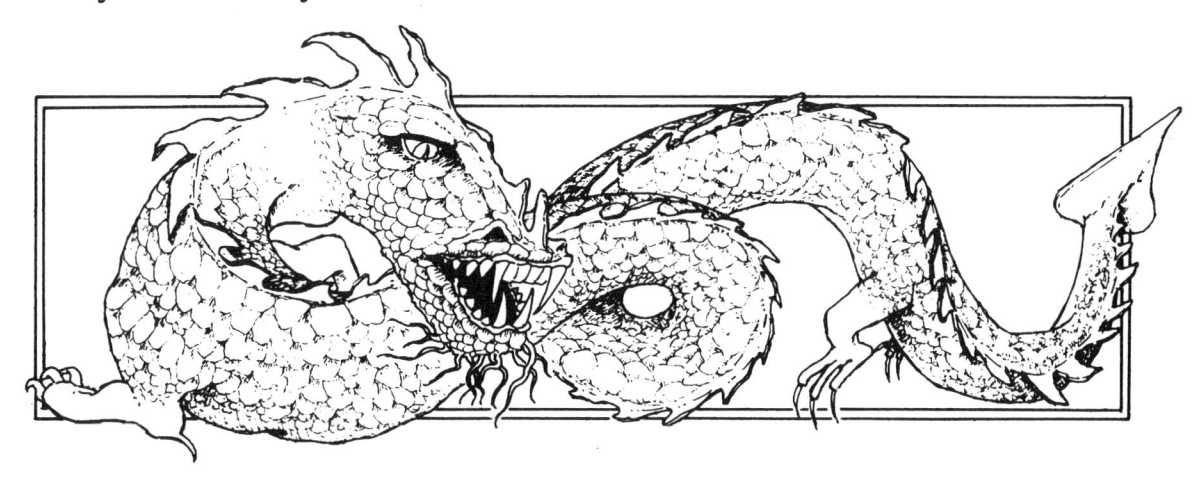

Homecoming

Author: Cynthia Voigt

Publisher, Date: Atheneum/Ballatine, 1981

Pages: 318

SUMMARY

The Tillerman children are abandoned by their mother in a shopping-mall parking lot near Cape Cod, Mass. Thirteen-year-old Dicey must take charge of her brothers, James and Sammy, and her sister, Maybeth. The only relative she knows of is a great-aunt living in Bridgeport, Conn., and so, with less than twenty dollars among them, the children set out on foot to find a relative none of them has ever met. When they finally reach Bridgeport, they discover that their great-aunt has died and her daughter is not prepared to provide a home for them. However, the children learn of their grandmother, who lives in Maryland, and set off again to find a home for themselves.

PRE-READING/MOTIVATIONAL ACTIVITIES

1. Locate Peewauket, Conn., where the story begins, on a map of the eastern United States. As the journey of the Tillermans unfolds, refer to the map to locate: Provincetown, Mass.; New Haven, Conn.; Bridgeport, Conn.; Wilmington, Del.; Annapolis, Md.; and Crisfield, Md.

2. Discuss what happens to children whose parents are unable to take care of them because of death, illness, or some other reason. (For example, they may live with foster parents or with other adults.) Bring out the fact that children from larger families may be separated from each other.

VOCABULARY/DISCUSSION QUESTIONS

Part 1, Chapters 1-4:

Vocabulary:

decipher (p. 10)	macadam (p. 24)
elaborated (p. 27)	raucous (p. 28)
sanctuary (p. 34)	pummeled (p. 35)
joists (p. 37)	flounces (p. 44)
incurious (p. 47)	promontories (p. 48)
silhouetted (p. 51)	loitering (p. 53)

Questions:

1. What do we know about each of the Tillermans by the end of chapter 4?

2. Why do you think Dicey decides that they should travel on their own to Bridgeport rather than get help from the police?

3. Reread page 24. Sammy's stubbornness is described in some detail, yet he agrees to do as Dicey asks and leaves the shopping center parking lot. Why?

4. On page 53 Sammy asks, "Are we runaways?" Are the children runaways? Explain.

Part 1, Chapters 5-8:

Vocabulary:

pluck the lotus (p. 65)
yacht (p. 85)
morbid (p. 87)
Dobro (p. 108)
clambered (p. 112)

laboriously (p. 69)
dinghy (p. 85)
resolutely (p. 88)
meandered (p. 111)

Questions:

1. Why does Dicey feel that the world is arranged for adults who have money? (p. 65)

2. The Tillermans and Louis and Edie are alike in that they are all runaways. How are they different?

3. How could Dicey be both angry at and proud of Sammy when he stole the food? (p. 87)

4. How does Dicey see herself? (p. 103) Do you agree?

5. "Never had she enjoyed a meal more," thought Dicey as the Tillermans ate at the diner with Windy. (p. 107) Why is this meal so enjoyable to her?

6. Prediction: What do you think lies ahead for the Tillermans?

Part 1, Chapters 9-12:

Vocabulary:

stoops (p. 116)
spiritual counselor (p. 120)
siblings (p. 123)
quelled (p. 131)
Bunsen burner (p. 134)

pursed (lips) (p. 117)
turbulence (p. 122)
resourceful (p. 128)
unemployment compensation (p. 134)
catechism (p. 135)

(vocabulary continues on next page)

lingerie (p. 136)
droned (p. 136)
conjecture (p. 143)
pawn shop (p. 147)
grace (state of) (p. 150)
substantial (p. 151)
legal guardian (p. 151)
cowl (p. 157)

quality control (p. 136)
fatigue (p. 139)
resilience (p. 144)
squeegee (p. 147)
preliminary arrangements (p. 151)
vocation (p. 151)
biddable (p. 152)
catatonic (p. 162)

Questions:

1. Once they arrive at Cousin Eunice's, Dicey feels sad for the first time in the book. Why now? (p. 121)

2. On page 135 James and Dicey talk about what makes each of them happy. James wants a good school and Dicey wants the ocean, lots of room outdoors, and food for the family. What do you think would make Eunice, Sammy, and Maybeth happy?

3. Why do you think Eunice keeps reminding Dicey about the sacrifices she has had to make for the children?

4. Why does earning money make Dicey so happy? (p. 146)

5. Why does Dicey trust Father Joseph? (p. 152)

6. Dicey seems very determined to go to Crisfield by herself, but gives in readily when the others insist on going along with her. Why?

Part 2, Chapters 1-4:

Vocabulary:

tenuous (p. 173)
grimace (p. 173)
odds and evens (p. 176)
bulkhead (p. 183)
masts (p. 186)
burnished (p. 186)
splicing (p. 190)
tack (p. 200)
boom (p. 200)
tiller (p. 201)
genoa sail (p. 202)
buoys (p. 206)

exhilarated (p. 173)
quelled (p. 176)
circuitous (p. 178)
rigging (p. 185)
spars (p. 186)
hull (p. 190)
berth (p. 192)
mainsail (p. 200)
keel (p. 200)
jib (p. 201)
quiet desperation (p. 204)
mottled (p. 217)

Questions:

1. From what you know about the Tillermans, why do you think they never had many friends? (p. 195)

2. How does James' view of what makes a family differ from Dicey's? (p. 196) Why do you think this is?

3. Why is Dicey so exhilarated by sailing? (pp. 202-203)

4. Even after the disappointing experience at Cousin Eunice's, the Tillermans are quite hopeful that things are going to be better at their grandmother's. Why?

Part 2, Chapters 5-8.

Vocabulary:

loblollies (p. 237)
veranda (p. 247)
traipsing (p. 255)
sailed close to the wind (p. 269)
reverie (p. 239)
burgeoned (p. 247)
painter (rope) (p. 256)

Questions:

1. Why don't the Tillermans stay with the circus?

2. What do we learn about their grandmother in these chapters?

3. What has their grandmother done so far that makes Dicey think she doesn't want them to leave? (p. 272)

Part 2, Chapters 9-12:

Vocabulary:

contradictions (p. 272)
bootlegging (p. 286)
proliferate (p. 275)

Questions:

1. What do you think Dicey means when she says her grandmother is a good enemy? (p. 294) What is a good enemy?

2. Grandmother tells Dicey that she is a fighter. Why do you think that Dicey is a fighter when neither of her parents were? (p. 301)

3. Why does Dicey find the late-night conversation with her grandmother so reassuring? (p. 302)

4. Why does their grandmother tell the children they can't stay?

5. Why do you think their grandmother changes her mind about letting the children stay?

Questions about the book in general:

1. When does James stop saying, "It's still true"? Why does he stop at this point in the story?

2. Why do you think the author titled this book "Homecoming"? (p. 90)

3. Why is the book divided into two parts?

4. Why do you think the author chose pairs of boys to help the Tillermans on their journey?

5. On a continuum ranging from helpful to harmful, where would you place each of the characters encountered by the Tillermans?

RELATED BOOKS

Other books about the Tillermans:
    Dicey's Song, 1982.
    A Solitary Blue, 1983.
    The Runner, 1985.
    Come a Stranger, 1986.
    Sons from Afar, 1987.
    Seventeen against the Dealer, 1989.

Adkins, Jan. *The Craft of Sail.* New York: Walker, 1973.

Cleaver, Vera, and Bill Cleaver. *Trial Valley.* New York: Lippincott, 1977.

_____. *Where the Lilies Bloom.* New York: Lippincott, 1969.

Gibbs, Tony. *Sailing.* New York: Watts, 1974.

Paterson, Katherine. *Jacob Have I Loved.* New York: Crowell, 1980.

Pickthall, Barry. *A Color Guide to Sailing.* Maidenhead, England: Chartwell Books, 1980; dist. by Book Sales, Secaucus, N.J.

Voigt, Cynthia. *Building Blocks.* New York: Atheneum, 1984.

_____. *Callender Papers.* New York: Atheneum, 1983.

_____. *Izzy, Willy-Nilly.* New York: Atheneum, 1986.

———. *Jackaroo.* New York: Atheneum, 1985.

———. *Tree by Leaf.* New York: Atheneum, 1988.

Wolf, Bernard. *Amazing Grace: Smith Island and the Chesapeake Watermen.* New York: Macmillan, 1986.

ENRICHMENT ACTIVITIES

Homecoming

1. Draw a map of the Tillermans' journey. Indicate locations of the important events and people in the story, such as the shopping center and where they meet the circus.

2. Draw a sailboat and label all of the parts. Explain to the group the function of the major parts, using your illustration as a visual aid.

3. Interview a social worker. Find out what happens to abandoned or homeless children in your community. Report your findings to the group.

4. Write a diary entry that each of the Tillermans might have written during their stay at Cousin Eunice's.

5. Draw an aerial view of grandmother's farm and the surrounding area.

6. Look at a map of your state. Make a chart showing how long it would take you to go from your community to several other locations by car (going 50 miles per hour) and by foot (going 10 miles per day).

7. Read *Where the Lilies Bloom*. Compare the situations of the Tillermans and the Luthers. How are they alike and different?

8. Read *Dicey's Song* or another of Cynthia Voigt's sequels to *Homecoming*.

9. Create your own activity for *Homecoming*.

Homesick: My Own Story

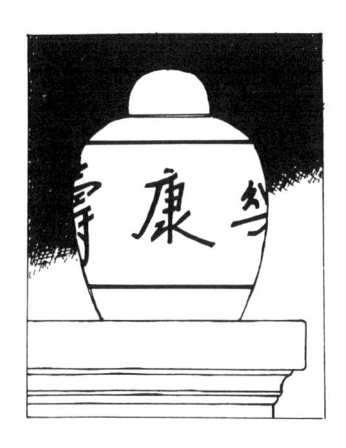

Author: Jean Fritz

Illustrator: Margot Tomes

Publisher, Date: Putnam, 1982

Pages: 163

SUMMARY

This book is an autobiography by an author who spent the first 12 years of her life in China. This book covers the years 1925 to 1927, when there was great civil unrest in China and Jean was anticipating her family's move back to the United States.

PRE-READING/MOTIVATIONAL ACTIVITIES

1. Ask the students to read the title and look at the picture on the cover of the book. Ask them these questions:
    What do you think the story is going to be about?
    Who do you think the main characters are going to be?
    What do you think is the setting of the story?

2. Look at a map of China. Locate the Yangtse River, Hankow, and Shanghai. If possible, locate and discuss pictures of China in the 1920s to familiarize students with the setting of the book.

3. Read "The Lay of the Last Minstral" Canto Six by Sir Walter Scott. discuss its meaning with the group. (*See* Related Books)

4. Look in an encyclopedia for a concise account of Chinese history. Read and discuss the information about the early 1900s.

5. Before reading the first section of the book, look up *YMCA* in an encyclopedia. Discuss reasons why the YMCA was located in China in the early 1900s.

VOCABULARY/DISCUSSION QUESTIONS

Chapters 1-2:

Vocabulary:

vividly (p. 7)	Hankow (p. 9)
Yangtse (p. 9)	River God (p. 9)
coolies (p. 9)	baton (p. 11)
prisoner's base (p. 11)	skittering (p. 12)
"bloody sorry" (p. 13)	French knots (p. 14)
amah (p. 14)	bound up feet (p. 17)
flustered (p. 18)	pagodas (p. 18)
"lose face" (p. 19)	concessions (p. 20)
the Bund (p. 20)	Customs House (p. 20)
promenade (p. 21)	Arabian Nights (p. 22)
junk (p. 23)	penknife (p. 24)
Shanghai (p. 24)	smallpox (p. 24)
"foreign devil" (p. 24)	dispensary (p. 26)
sauntered (p. 29)	lacquer (table) (p. 31)
middy blouse (p. 33)	ricksha (p. 33)
raspier (p. 39)	camomile (p. 40)
turret (p. 41)	withering look (p. 41)
Communists (p. 42)	warlord (p. 43)
doily (p. 43)	labor of love (p. 43)
missionary (p. 45)	dutifully (p. 47)
curtsy (p. 47)	

Questions:

1. Why do you think Jean is so determined not to sing "God Save the King" at school?

2. Why does she identify so strongly as an American when she has never been to the United States?

3. Why does Jean take out her frustrations with school on Lin Nai-Nai? (pp. 14-17)

4. Jean describes Chinese characters in the following way: "Chinese words don't march across flat surfaces the way ours do; they drop down cliffs, one cliff after another from right to left across a page." (p. 18) What does this tell you about her opinion of the two cultures?

5. What does it mean to "lose face"? Why would Yang Sze-Fu lose face if his carved butter pagoda was sent back to the kitchen? (p. 19) Why do you think a coolie was willing to run himself to death so that he wouldn't lose face? (p. 34)

6. Why do the British put up a sign that says, "NO DOGS, NO CHINESE"?

7. Why do you think Jean carves her name on the boat? (p. 24)

8. Why doesn't Jean want to be "good"? (p. 30)

9. Why do you think the Hulls are so secretive about David's adoption and birth parents when they are so open about other subjects? (pp. 33-37)

10. "Andrea and I were used to being called 'foreign devil.' We were used to insults. Coolies often spat directly in our path, but we had been taught to act as if we didn't see, as if nothing had happened." (p. 42) Why had they been taught to respond that way? What does this say about their attitudes toward the Chinese?

11. David, Andrea, and Jean all have their own reasons for wanting Millie to come for Christmas. What are they? Why is Millie so unhappy about being there?

12. Why does the name Marjorie appeal to Jean? Why does she think things would be different if her name was Marjorie?

Chapters 3-4:

Vocabulary:

revolution (p. 53)
strikes (p. 53)
agitators (p. 53)
riot (p. 54)
hair bobbed (p. 56)
Kuling (p. 58)
Kiukiang (p. 62)
phlebitis (p. 68)
Panama hat (p. 78)
refugees (p. 78)
capitalist (p. 86)
siege (p. 86)
whiz-bang (p. 91)
ablative (case) (p. 92)
spit curls (p. 99)

demonstrations (p. 53)
marches (p. 53)
haranguing (p. 53)
upheaval (p. 55)
Peitaiho (p. 57)
sedan chair (p. 59)
azaleas (p. 65)
Wuchang (p. 77)
white duck (cloth) (p. 78)
potassium (p. 84)
flourish (p. 86)
skirmish (p. 90)
dative (case) (p. 92)
relief (p. 92)

Questions:

1. What is a riot? Find a definition of *riot* in a reference book. Why are riots breaking out in Hankow?

2. Why do you think Jean's parents are so secretive about important family events, such as having a baby (p. 69) and changing summer vacation plans? (pp. 58-59)

3. Read the paragraph at the bottom of page 61. Why do you think Jean is so attracted to the river?

4. Why does Jean feel so misunderstood?

5. How does seeing Yang Sze-Fu in the courtyard convince Jean that he was not trying to poison the family? (p. 86)

6. Why does Jean's mother declare a "school holiday" the day that Jean's father and Lin Nai-Nai went to Wuchang? (p. 94)

7. Why do you think Jean's mother won't talk about Miriam? (p. 95)

8. How do Lin Nai-Nai's experiences in Wuchang change Jean's feelings toward her? (pp. 96-97)

Chapters 5-7:

Vocabulary:

Nationalist (p. 100)
Nanking (p. 103)
consulate (p. 107)
sophisticated (p. 116)
knickers (p. 125)
Charles Lindbergh (p. 132)
smearcase (p. 140)

Charleston (p. 102)
scuttling (p. 106)
emergency procedures (p. 108)
pirouetting (p. 117)
dire (p. 131)
flannel cakes (p. 137)
"get exercised" (p. 149)

Questions:

1. Reread the last three paragraphs on page 101. Why is Jean crying?

2. Reread the fourth paragraph on page 103. What does this tell you about Jean's father?

3. Why is Jean's mother suddenly so interested in Jean's appearance? (pp. 111-112)

4. Jean thinks, "She (Andrea) knew just how to get ready for life while all I seemed to do was to wait for life to happen." (p. 115) How are Jean and Andrea different?

5. Reread the first full paragraph on page 122. What do you think Jean is trying to tell David about their past?

6. Reread the paragraph beginning, "Well, I knew exactly what it would be like . . ." on page 125. Do you think Jean has a realistic view of what school in America would be like?

7. Why does Jean find finally arriving in America so disconcerting? (p. 131)

8. When does she finally feel at home?

9. How is Jean's relationship with her grandmother different from her relationship with her mother? (pp. 146-147)

10. Reread page 149. Why do you think Andrew Carr whispered that rhyme to Jean?

11. Was Jean's first day of school in America what she thought it would be? Explain.

12. Why do you think the author ends the story where she does?

13. View and discuss the filmstrip *Unlearning Asian American Stereotypes* (*see* Other Materials). Do you think *Homesick: My Own Story* confirms or contradicts Asian stereotypes? Explain.

14. Look at Margot Tomes' illustrations. How does the artwork reflect the text? Why do you think the artist chose to illustrate those particular events in the story? Which events would you have chosen to illustrate?

RELATED BOOKS

Archer, Jules. *The Chinese and the Americans.* New York: Hawthorn Books, 1976.

Barlow, Jeffrey. *Sun Yat-Sen.* New York: Chelsea House, 1987.

Dolan, Sean. *Chiang Kai-shek.* New York: Chelsea House, 1988.

Dunster, Jack, *China and Mao Zedong.* Minneapolis, Minn.: Lerner, 1983.

Fritz, Jean. *And Then What Happened, Paul Revere?* New York: Putnam, 1973.

_____. *Brendan the Navigator.* New York: Putnam, 1979.

_____. *The Cabin Faced West.* New York: Putnam, 1958.

_____. *Can't You Make Them Behave, King George?* New York: Putnam, 1982.

_____. *China Homecoming.* New York: Putnam, 1985.

_____. *China's Long March: 6000 Miles of Danger.* New York: Putnam, 1988.

_____. *The Double Life of Pocohantas.* New York: Putnam, 1983.

_____. *George Washington's Breakfast.* New York: Putnam, 1969.

_____. *Make Way for Sam Houston.* New York: Putnam, 1986.

_____. *The Man Who Loved Books.* New York: Putnam, 1981.

_____. *Shh! We're Writing the Constitution.* New York: Putnam, 1987.

_____. *Stonewall.* New York: Putnam, 1979.

_____. *Traitor: The Case of Benedict Arnold.* New York: Putnam, 1981.

_____. *What's the Big Idea, Ben Franklin?* New York: Putnam, 1982.

_____. *Where Do You Think You're Going, Christopher Columbus?* New York: Putnam, 1980.

_____. *Where Was Patrick Henry on the 29th of May?* New York: Putnam, 1975.

_____. *Who's That Stepping on Plymouth Rock?* New York: Putnam, 1975.

_____. *Why Don't You Get a Horse, Sam Adams?* New York: Putnam, 1974.

_____. *Will You Sign Here, John Hancock?* New York: Putnam, 1976.

Garza, Hedda. *Mao Zedong.* New York: Chelsea House, 1988.

Gibbon, David. *China: A Picture Book to Remember Her By.* London: Crescent, 1979.

Goldsmith-Carter, George. *Sailing Ships and Sailing Craft.* New York: Grosset & Dunlap, 1970.

Lewis, John. *The Chinese Word for Horse.* New York: Two Continents, 1976.

Loescher, Gil. *China: Pushing toward the Year 2000.* New York: Harcourt Brace Jovanovich, 1981.

McLenighan, Valjean. *China: A History to 1949.* Chicago: Children's Press, 1983.

Miller, Irene Preston. *The Stitchery Book: Embroidery for Beginners.* Garden City, N.Y.: Doubleday, 1965.

Paludan, Lis. *Easy Embroidery.* New York: Taplinger, 1975.

Roberson, John R. *China: From Manchu to Mao (1699-1976).* New York: Atheneum, 1980.

Robottom, John. *China in Revolution.* New York: McGraw-Hill, 1969.

Scott, Sir Walter. *The Complete Poetical Works of Sir Walter Scott.* New York: Thomas Y. Crowell, 1984.

Wolff, Diane. *Chinese Writing: An Introduction.* New York: Holt, Rinehart & Winston, 1975.

OTHER MATERIALS

Unlearning Asian American Stereotypes: A Filmstrip and Discussion Guide. New York: Council on Interracial Books for Children, 1982.
Available from
   Council on Interracial Books for Children
   1841 Broadway
   New York, NY 10023

ENRICHMENT ACTIVITIES

Homesick: My Own Story

1. Research nineteenth-century Chinese history. Find out why Americans, Europeans, and Russians were in China at that time. Take notes and report your findings to the group.

2. Do biographical sketches of Sun Yat-sen, Chiang Kai-shek, and Mao Tse-tung. Make sure to include their activities from 1925-27, the time period in which this book takes place.

3. Symbols of American patriotism were very important to Jean. Make up a patriotic quiz of American symbols, songs, etc., for example: What are the words to the Pledge of Allegiance? How many stripes and stars are on our flag? What is the national bird? Who wrote the words to "The Star Spangled Banner"? Administer the quiz to at least 10 children and adults. Score the quizzes and graph the results.

4. Research the role of foreign missionaries in China in the early 1900s. Why were they there? What kind of work did they do? How many were there? Where did they come from?

5. Read *China Homecoming*, the sequel to *Homesick: My Own Story*, or another book by Jean Fritz.

6. Learn at least five embroidery stitches and use them to make an original picture or design. You will need embroidery floss, a piece of fabric, a needle, and an embroidery hoop.

7. Write a letter that Jean might have written to Lin Nai-Nai after her first day of school in the United States.

8. Make a labeled drawing or model of a Chinese junk.

9. Read *Chinese Writing: An Introduction*, by Diane Wolff, or *The Chinese Word for Horse*, by John Lewis. Use large brushes and ink blocks to paint Chinese characters.

10. Find someone who speaks Chinese or listen to a Chinese language tape. Learn how to say some simple phrases in Chinese.

11. Locate, memorize, and recite canto 6, stanza 1 of "The Lay of the Last Minstrel" by Sir Walter Scott.

12. Create your own activity for *Homesick: My Own Story*.

Nobody's Family Is Going to Change

Author: Louise Fitzhugh

Publisher, Date: Farrar, Straus, Giroux, 1974

Pages: 221

SUMMARY

Twelve-year-old Emma Sheridan wants to be a lawyer when she grows up. Her younger brother, Willie, has his heart set on a stage career as a dancer. Their father is vehemently opposed to both their plans, but he has not taken into account his children's determination and the power of the secret Children's Army to change even the most hardened situation.

PRE-READING/MOTIVATIONAL ACTIVITIES

1. Read pages 3-5 aloud to the group. Discuss what they learned about Willie and Emma and their relationship from this passage.

2. If the students are unfamiliar with large city life, show them pictures of New York City. Be sure to include residential areas as well as business and tourist areas.

3. Go over the specialized vocabulary for dance and law. Have a student or parent who has taken dance lessons demonstrate some of the steps mentioned in the book. You may be able to find a video that contains information about dance steps. Familiarize the group with basic information about courtroom procedure and the legal system (*see* Related Books).

4. Look at the publication date of the book (1974). Sex segregation in occupations was more common then than it is now. Discuss occupations such as lawyer, doctor, or dentist that were considered to be professions for men only.

VOCABULARY/DISCUSSION QUESTIONS

Legal Vocabulary:

habeas corpus (p. 4)
district attorney (p. 16)
cross-examining (p. 19)
accusation (p. 20)
Bar Association (p. 23)
Bill of Rights (p. 27)

brief (p. 6)
bar exam (p. 18)
torts (p. 20)
heinous crime (p. 21)
Magna Carta (p. 27)
Constitution (p. 27)

(vocabulary continues on next page)

Declaration of Independence (p. 27)
contracts (p. 37)
bailiffs (p. 54)
dissenting (p. 86)
amicus curiae (p. 97)
hearsay (p. 135)
contempt of court (p. 142)
defense lawyer (p. 161)
badgering the witness (p. 161)
confer (p. 163)
plead a mistrial (p. 165)
incarcerated (p. 166)
due process (p. 166)
pursuit of happiness (p. 168)

maltreatment (p. 31)
Merck Manual (p. 38)
children's rights (p. 55)
harassments (p. 87)
litigation (p. 124)
continuance (p. 142)
adoption (p. 155)
objection (p. 161)
leading the witness (p. 162)
begging the indulgence of the court (p. 163)
complainant (p. 165)
jury (p. 166)
undue influence (p. 167)

Dance Vocabulary:

shuffle-ball-change (p. 3)
soft shoe (p. 3)
hop-shuffle (p. 3)
riff (p. 4)
tap shoes (p. 5)
breaks (p. 5)
high chorus walk (p. 9)
vaudeville exit (p. 13)
shay (p. 13)
footlights (p. 16)
ragtime (p. 60)
producer (p. 62)
cakewalk (p. 61)
audition (p. 63)
Equity Card (p. 131)
shtick (p. 200)
down-stage (p. 200)
stage right (p. 200)

flaps (p. 3)
cut time (p. 3)
pullbacks (p. 4)
buck-and-wing (p. 4)
show time step (p. 5)
pirouetted (p. 9)
in stock (p. 11)
hoofers (p. 13)
summer stock (p. 16)
minstrel show (p. 48)
director (p. 62)
press agent (p. 62)
shuffle (p. 61)
agent (p. 131)
take five (p. 200)
piece of business (p. 200)
up-stage (p. 200)
stage left (p. 200)

People and Places Vocabulary:

East End (p. 4)
Broadway (p. 10)
Fred Astaire (p. 15)
Bill Robinson (p. 15)
Sidney Poitier (p. 34)
Borough of Manhattan (p. 54)
Anne Frank (p. 64)
Peter Jensen (p. 64)
Zsa Zsa Gabor (p. 66)
Golda Meir (p. 98)

Bronx Zoo (p. 4)
Ted Mack Hour (p. 13)
Donald O'Connor (p. 15)
Nijinsky (p. 29)
Gloria Steinem (p. 35)
Scott Joplin (p. 60)
Oliver Twist (p. 64)
Prague (p. 66)
French Underground (p. 74)
Simone de Beauvoir (p. 98)

Page 3-55:

Vocabulary:

simultaneously (p. 3)	faggot (p. 4)
Afro (p. 4)	audacity (p. 4)
plaintively (p. 9)	gypsies (p. 9)
melodramatic (p. 10)	infuriated (p. 11)
Baltic origin (p. 15)	book satchel (p. 16)
go starkers (p. 16)	consumption (p. 17)
cream horn (p. 17)	Emancipation (p. 17)
dietician (p. 19)	jovially (p. 20)
ottoman (p. 20)	rape (p. 21)
forty-niner (p. 22)	ascension (p. 23)
complacently (p. 27)	tuxedo (p. 28)
nappy (p. 30)	booby hatch (p. 34)
women's liberation movement (p. 35)	male chauvinism (p. 36)
ineffectual (p. 36)	menstruation (p. 38)
no-count (p. 45)	Depression (p. 47)
honkies (p. 47)	sarcasm (p. 53)
dumbfounded (p. 53)	spectacles (p. 55)

Questions:

1. Mr. Sheridan and Dipsey have very different opinions of male dancers. (pp. 8-10) Compare their points of view.

2. Do you think children like Emma and Willie would drive parents crazy? Explain your answer.

3. Why do you think Mr. Sheridan is so cold toward Emma when she asks legal questions? (pp. 20-22)

4. Why do you think Willie and Emma are so focused on careers at such an early age?

5. Why do you think Emma is so intent on hurting Willie? (pp. 28-32)

6. Do you think Emma's name is really Emancipation, or did she choose that name for herself? (p. 17)

7. Why does Emma tell her father that she's going to be a doctor when she has no intention of becoming one? (p. 43)

8. Why do you think Emma eats so much?

9. Why does Mrs. Sheridan laugh when Emma tells her she wants to be a lawyer? (pp. 51-52)

10. Prediction: Reread the last full paragraph on page 55. What do you think Emma will do?

210 / Nobody's Family Is Going to Change

Pages 55-107:

Vocabulary:

monitor (p. 58)	segregated (p. 64)
delicatessen (p. 66)	revolutionaries (p. 66)
reactionary (p. 66)	capitalist (p. 66)
pacifist (p. 68)	deluded (p. 69)
tic (face) (p. 71)	gruesome (p. 71)
contorted (p. 71)	gyration (p. 71)
political convention (p. 73)	Gauloise-smoking (p. 74)
essence (p. 74)	movement (cause) (p. 74)
ramifications (p. 75)	power salute (p. 75)
podium (p. 77)	battered child (p. 78)
barbaric (p. 79)	confiscating (p. 79)
Braille (p. 81)	mortified (p. 81)
speech impediment (p. 83)	traipsing (p. 94)
fathom (p. 98)	pickaninny (p. 106)

Questions:

1. Why does Willie leave school to go to Dipsey's apartment when he knows his parents will disapprove?

2. Why do you think Emma has such a difficult time choosing cookies to take to the meeting? (pp. 66-67)

3. "At all times, whenever confronted, each member of this Army must and will say that he or she is only acting out of personal feeling and friendship for the child involved." (p. 79) Why is this an effective tactic? What does it accomplish?

4. "Numbers are what we rely on, and the embarrassment of parents when caught by children. It almost always works." (p. 86) How does embarrassment of parents work as a tactic to change their behavior toward their children? (pp. 80-81)

5. Why does Emma have a difficult time joining the Children's Army even though she believes in what they are doing? (pp. 85-90)

6. How is Willie and Emma's relationship changing? Why? (pp. 106-107)

7. How are the four girls (Emma, Goldin, Ketchum, and Saunders) alike? How are they different?

8. Prediction: Do you think the Children's Army is going to help Willie? Explain.

Pages 107-155:

Vocabulary:

inexplicably (p. 109)
transvestitism (p. 114)
alacrity (p. 143)
indecent proposals (p. 112)
magnanimously (p. 142)

Questions:

1. Why are Ketchum and the other girls so frightened that the Children's Army will come to their houses? (p. 113)

2. Why do you think Emma begins to feel guilty for the way she has been treating Willie? (p. 119)

3. Why does Emma feel dissatisfied after the meeting in the park? (p. 133)

4. Why is Emma focusing her anger on her mother instead of her father? (p. 134)

5. "She tried not to see it, but she had to: she was trying to hate Willie again so she wouldn't have to face this thing." (p. 138) What does this passage mean?

6. Why is Mrs. Sheridan starting to side with Willie against his father? (p. 139)

7. Why isn't Dipsey willing to confront Mr. Sheridan about Willie's dancing on Broadway?

8. Why do you think Willie is the only one in the family who is not afraid of Mr. Sheridan? (p. 151)

9. Why does Mrs. Sheridan always say, "We'll see"?

10. Prediction: Will Willie get to stay in the show? Describe what you think will happen.

Pages 155-End:

Vocabulary:

timorously (p. 168)
mobilize (p. 187)
sepulchral voice (p. 198)
leprechauns (p. 214)
surreptitiously (p. 216)
condescending (p. 187)
countermanded (p. 191)
changling (p. 214)
inarticulate (p. 215)
consciousness-raising group (p. 217)

Questions:

1. Do you think Emma hurt or helped Willie's cause when she took on the role of his attorney? (pp. 161-168)

2. Why does Mr. Sheridan refuse to change even when his whole family disagrees with him?

3. Does Mr. Sheridan really hate Emma? (p. 175) Explain.

4. "Spoiled! That's a word you made up to make yourself feel better." (p. 174) What does Emma mean when she says this?

5. Why is it hard for Emma to think about her mother? Why doesn't she want to know what her mother thinks of her? (p. 179)

6. How are cases chosen for the Children's Army to act upon? (pp. 183-188) Why don't Emma's complaint or her friends' complaints qualify?

7. What does Mr. Sheridan mean when he says, "It's you who's the father, in Willie's mind"? (p. 191) Do you agree with him? Explain.

8. Why do you think Mr. Sheridan has been so intent on "besting" Emma since she was a child? (pp. 193-194)

9. Reread pages 205-206. Why do all of these disturbing thoughts leave Emma feeling peaceful?

10. Why does Emma feel better once she decides that her parents aren't going to change? (pp. 211-214)

11. At what point in the story do Emma and Willie finally become united? (p. 182) Why?

12. Find out more about Changelings. Why is this a good name for their group?

13. Why do you think Emma pushes the chocolate cake away? (p. 221)

14. Prediction: What do you think Emma is going to do?

15. Do you agree with the title?

RELATED BOOKS

Archer, Jules. *Who's Running Your Life? A Look at Young People's Rights.* New York: Harcourt Brace Jovanovich, 1979.

Brindze, Ruth. *All about Courts and the Law.* New York: Random House, 1964.

Carlson, Dale. *Girls Are Equal, Too: The Women's Movement for Teenagers.* New York: Atheneum, 1973.

Coughlin, George G. *Here Is Your Career: The Law.* New York: Putnam, 1979.

Epstein, Sam, and Beryl Epstein. *Kids in Court: The ACLU Defends Their Rights.* New York: Four Winds, 1982.

Fitzhugh, Louise. *Harriet the Spy.* New York: Harper & Row, 1964.

———. *The Long Secret.* New York: Harper & Row, 1965.

———. *Sport.* New York: Harper & Row, 1979.

Goldreich, Gloria, and Esther Goldreich. *What Can She Be? A Lawyer.* New York: Lothrop, Lee & Shepard, 1973.

Haskins, Jim. *Your Rights, Past and Present: A Guide for Young People.* New York: Hawthorn Books, 1975.

Horton, Louise, *Careers in Theatre, Music and Dance.* New York: Watts, 1976.

Kohn, Bernice. *'The Spirit and the Letter': The Struggle for Rights in America.* New York: Viking, 1974.

Komisar, Lucy. *The New Feminism.* New York: Watts, 1971.

Krementz, Jill. *A Very Young Dancer.* New York: Knopf, 1976.

Kuklin, Susan. *Reaching for Dreams: A Ballet from Rehearsal to Opening Night.* New York: Lothrop, Lee & Shepard, 1987.

Loeb, Robert. *Your Legal Rights as a Minor,* revised ed. New York: Watts, 1978.

Sarnoff, Paul. *Careers in the Legal Profession.* New York: Julian Messner, 1970.

Splarer, Sarah. *Non-traditional Careers for Women.* New York: Julian Messner, 1973.

Swiger, Elinor Porter. *The Law and You: A Handbook for Young People.* Indianapolis: Bobbs-Merrill, 1973.

Tobias, Tobi. *Arthur Mitchell.* New York: Crowell, 1975.

Zeck, Gerry. *I Love to Dance.* Minneapolis, Minn.: Carolrhoda Books, 1982.

ENRICHMENT ACTIVITIES

Nobody's Family Is Going to Change

1. View the film *The Tap Dance Kid*. Compare the film to the book. Which do you think is more effective.

2. Reread the description of Emma's room on pages 97-98. Design a room for Willie. Design a room for yourself.

3. Write a Children's Bill of Rights.

4. If Martha kept a diary or wrote a letter to a friend, what would she say about events in the book? Write your ideas in the form of a letter or diary.

5. Invite a lawyer or other legal expert to come to your class to talk about children's rights. Write a list of questions to help guide the discussion.

6. Read another book by Louise Fitzhugh.

7. Do research and write a report on one or more women who were pioneers in a previously male-only profession, such as:
   - Sally Ride
   - Belva Lockwood
   - Sandra Day O'Connor
   - Jeannette Rankin
   - Shirley Chisholm
   - Elizabeth Blackwell
   - Marie Curie

8. On page 75, the girl at the registration table tells Emma and the other girls the Children's Army's beliefs:
   "We believe that if every decision made on this earth were first put to the test of one question, 'Is this good for children?' and the decision makers were forced to make decisions that would be good for children, there would only be good decisions made."
   Do you agree or disagree with this statement? Write an essay explaining your point of view.

9. What does Willie have to look forward to in his career as a professional dancer? Read a biography of a professional dancer or a book about the world of professional dancing. Share what you learn with the group.

10. Research and write a report on one of the following historical topics mentioned in the story:
    History of tap dancing
    Women in the law profession
    Women's movement
    Civil rights movement
    Children's rights

11. Write and administer a survey of your classmates to determine their attitudes toward male dancers and female lawyers. You may want to extend this survey to include other examples of men and women in nontraditional occupations, such as male nurses or female construction workers. Graph your results and share the information with the group.

12. Interview several adults to find out what their career plans were as children and how these plans changed, or didn't change, as they got older.

13. Create your own activity for *Nobody's Family Is Going to Change*.

Roll of Thunder, Hear My Cry

Author: Mildred D. Taylor

Illustrator: Jerry Pinkney

Publisher, Date: Dial, 1976

Pages: 276

SUMMARY

This story takes place in rural Mississippi at the height of the Depression. The Logans are the only black family to own land in the immediate area, and there are many white neighbors who would be glad to see them "go under." Nine-year-old Cassie Logan relates the events of the year in which her mother gets fired from her teaching job for standing up to the school board, her parents organize a boycott of the local general store, a young friend narrowly avoids being lynched, and Cassie and her brothers learn how to survive racial discrimination with strength and courage. This realistic historical novel is a sequel to *Song of the Trees* (*see* page 118).

PRE-READING/MOTIVATIONAL ACTIVITIES

1. You may want to read the prequel, *Song of the Trees*, to the group. This book sets the scene for *Roll of Thunder, Hear My Cry*.

2. Discuss the realities of race relations in the South prior to the modern civil rights movement. Show the students photos that illustrate the institutional racial segregation that preceded the movement (*see* Related Books). Discuss the different experiences that black children and white children would have had at that time.

3. Discuss what life is like for poor families living in rural areas (*see* Related Books). Be sure to include reliance on homegrown food, transportation difficulties, limited job opportunities, limited public funds for education and public welfare, and a lower standard of living for everyone.

4. Ask the students to read the title and look at the picture on the cover of the book. Ask them these questions:
    What do you think the story is going to be about?
    Who do you think the main characters are going to be?
    What do you think is the setting of the story? If students are unfamiliar with the rural South, show them pictures of this part of the country.

5. Discuss the Ku Klux Klan and its role in maintaining racial segregation. Related words and phrases such as lynched, tar and feather, night men, and "They're riding tonight," are mentioned in the story.

VOCABULARY/DISCUSSION QUESTIONS

Chapters 1-2:

Vocabulary:

oil sausages (p. 3)	meticulously (p. 3)
concession (p. 4)	intriguing (p. 4)
disposition (p. 4)	raucous (p. 5)
pensively (p. 6)	undaunted (p. 8)
morosely (p. 11)	gullies (p. 12)
knell (p. 15)	buckeyed (p. 18)
tarpaulin (p. 19)	dubious (p. 21)
unveiling (p. 21)	audible (p. 22)
noncommital (p. 29)	composition (p. 29)
maverick (p. 30)	imperious (p. 31)
chiffonier (p. 36)	lynched (p. 40)

Questions:

1. What do we know about each of the characters: the Logan children, T. J., Claude, Jeremy, Big Ma, Mama, and Papa?

2. What do Miss Crocker and Mama's different attitudes toward the textbooks reveal about them?

3. Compare and contrast: What is the general attitude of the white characters toward black people? What is the general attitude of the black characters toward white people? Use specific examples from the story.

4. Why do you think Papa brings Mr. Morrison home to live on the farm?

Chapters 3-4:

Explain to the group the sharecropping system; the relationship between farm owners, sharecroppers, and local stores; and buying on credit and paying your bills when the crop comes in.

Vocabulary:

drastic (p. 50)	stealthily (p. 50)
oblivious (p. 51)	night men (p. 62)
ploy (p. 74)	engrossed (p. 85)

Questions:

1. Why doesn't Stacey like Mr. Morrison at first?

2. Why did the Logan children find the bus incident so amusing?

3. How will Mama's plans to shop at the Vicksburg stores upset the unjust sharecropping system?

4. What does "backed your signature" and "signed for me" mean? (pp. 99-100)

5. Prediction: What do you think will happen next?

Chapters 5-6:

Vocabulary:

subdued (p. 103)
promenade (p. 107)
haughtily (p. 109)
malevolently (p. 112)
faltered (p. 115)
retaliated (p. 129)

clabber milk (p. 106)
veranda (p. 107)
mercantile (p. 109)
wryly (p. 113)
reprimand (p. 125)
chignon (p. 131)

Questions:

1. Why does Big Ma take the kids to Strawberry this particular day? (pp. 102-103)

2. Why hadn't Big Ma ever taken the kids to Strawberry before? (pp. 102-103)

3. Why do you think T. J. is so fascinated by the pearl-handled gun?

4. Why doesn't Cassie understand the racial discrimination at the market and in the Barnett Mercantile?

5. Why does Big Ma insist that Cassie apologize to Lillian Jean Simms?

6. How do the different members of Cassie's family react to her encounters with Mr. Barnett and the Simmses?

7. How do Mama and Uncle Hammer's views differ? Why?

Roll of Thunder, Hear My Cry / 219

Chapters 7-8:

Vocabulary:

admonished (p. 141)
stageworthy (p. 147)
breeding stock (p. 149)
aristocracy (p. 159)
candidly (p. 161)
revenue (p. 163)
citified (p. 166)
condoned (p. 168)
Uncle Tomming (p. 173)
sentinels (p. 175)
economic cycle (p. 183)
tenant farming (p. 187)

encounter (p. 143)
Reconstruction (p. 147)
collateral (p. 152)
placid (p. 160)
eviction (p. 163)
bootlegging whiskey (p. 166)
insolently (p. 168)
carpetbaggers (p. 169)
feigned (p. 174)
sauntered (p. 179)
generated (p. 183)

Questions:

1. Why does Stacey give T. J. his coat?

2. Why do you think Jeremy wants to be Stacey's friend?

3. Why is it okay for Papa to be friends with Mr. Jamison but not okay for Stacey to be friends with Jeremy?

4. Why is Mr. Jamison backing the credit for the sharecroppers who want to do their shopping in Vicksburg?

5. Why do you think Mr. Granger comes to talk to the Logans?

6. Why is Cassie's plan for getting even with Lillian Jean Simms a good one? How did she come up with such a plan?

7. If teaching is so important to Mama, why does she take such big chances?

8. Why does T. J. do the things he does in chapter 8?

Chapters 9-10:

Vocabulary:

amenities (p. 203)
analogy (p. 207)
shroud (p. 227)
revival (p. 233)

fig tree (p. 206)
despondently (p. 223)
lethargically (p. 227)

Questions:

1. Why do Papa and Mr. Morrison go to Vicksburg even though most of the other families have gone back to shopping at the Wallace Store?

2. Why do you think Papa takes Stacey with him to Vicksburg? (pp. 206-208)

3. Why do the Wallaces wait for night to attack?

4. Why does T. J. bring the Simmses to the revival? Why do you think the Simmses want to come?

Chapters 11-12:

Vocabulary:

   traipsing (p. 258)
   adamant (p. 258)

Questions:

1. Why does T. J. turn to the Logans for help when he is hurt?

2. Why do you think Stacey risks so much to help T. J.?

3. What is Harlan Granger's role in this community? Give examples.

4. Who are the night men who go to the Averys' house? Why do they treat the Averys the way they do?

5. Why can't the sheriff or Mr. Jamison stop the lynching?

6. Why is Papa's plan to keep the men from lynching T. J. such a good one?

7. Why do you think Cassie says she is crying for the land at the end of the story?

Questions about the book in general:

1. How do the different characters change throughout the course of the book?

2. How do each of these things contribute to the final events of the story:
    Stacey's new coat
    Uncle Hammer's car
    the school books
    the pearl-handled gun
    the cotton crop
    the Logan land

3. Why is *Roll of Thunder, Hear My Cry* a good title for the book?

RELATED BOOKS

Other books about the Logan family:
   Song of the Trees, 1975.
   Let the Circle Be Unbroken, 1981.
   The Friendship, 1987.
   The Road to Memphis, 1990.

Adoff, Arnold. *Celebrations: A New Anthology of Black American Poetry.* Chicago: Follett, 1977.

Boardman, Fon W. *The Thirties: America and the Great Depression.* New York: Henry Z. Walck, 1967.

Carruth, Ella Kaiser. *She Wanted to Read: The Story of Mary McLeod Bethune.* New York: Abingdon, 1969.

Cook, Fred J. *The Ku Klux Klan: America's Recurring Nightmare.* New York: Julian Messner, 1980.

Hunt, Irene. *No Promises in the Wind.* New York: Follett, 1970.

Lawson, Don. *FDR's New Deal.* New York: Crowell, 1979.

Lindop, Edmund. *Modern America: the Turbulent Thirties.* New York: Watts, 1970.

Meltzer, Milton, ed. *In Their Own Words: A History of the American Negro 1916-1966.* New York: Crowell, 1967.

Naylor, Phyllis Reynolds. *Walking through the Dark.* New York: Atheneum, 1976.

Taylor, Mildred D. *The Gold Cadillac.* New York: Dial, 1987.

ENRICHMENT ACTIVITIES

Roll of Thunder, Hear My Cry

1. Find out more about racial segregation in the rural South in the early 1930s. Write a report focusing on the inequality that existed at that time.

2. Research the Ku Klux Klan and its role in maintaining racial segregation. Trace the history of the organization to the present. Make a time line to help you share this information with the group.

3. Learn more about growing cotton and the sharecropping system. Draw a series of pictures to help you explain the system to the group.

4. Make a map of the Logan farm and the community around it.

5. At the beginning of chapter 11, Mr. Morrison sings the black spiritual, "Roll of Thunder," while he is guarding the house. Locate a book of black spirituals and find songs to represent the members of the Logan family. Make a display matching the characters and the song lyrics.

6. Cornbread was a staple in the Logan family's diet. On pages 198-199 Mama talks about using less flour and less baking powder because their food supplies were running low. Find a cornbread recipe. Make several batches using less flour and baking powder in each. What happens to the bread? How does it taste?

7. Write a news story about the final event in the book as it might have appeared in the local newspaper.

8. Write a letter that Cassie might have written to Uncle Hammer the day after the fire and T. J.'s arrest.

9. Mama had always wanted to be a teacher. Develop questions and interview several teachers to find out how and when they decided to go into teaching. Report your findings to the group.

10. Read another book by Mildred D. Taylor.

11. Create your own activity for *Roll of Thunder, Hear My Cry*.

Sing Down the Moon

Author: Scott O'Dell

Publisher, Date: Houghton Mifflin, 1970

Pages: 137

SUMMARY

This book takes place in the American Southwest from 1863 to 1865. The story is told by Bright Morning, a young Navaho girl who is kidnapped by Spanish slavers. She escapes and returns to her village shortly before the Navahos are evicted from their land and forced to walk three hundred miles to Fort Sumner, N.M., in what is now known as The Long Walk. In the final pages of the book, Bright Morning marries Tall Boy, her childhood sweetheart, and they eventually return to Navaho land.

PRE-READING/MOTIVATIONAL ACTIVITIES

1. Have the students find out where the Navahos, Hopis, Utes, Nez Perce, Zunis, Kiowas, and Apaches were located before 1865. Show this information on an outline map of the southwestern United States.

2. Show the students pictures of the natural landscape of Arizona and New Mexico. Find examples of and discuss mesas, canyons, draws, barrancas, ravines, pinon trees, aspen groves, mesquite, cactus, sycamores, yucca, and hogans.

3. Read a brief description of the U.S. government's Indian policy in the mid-1800s and its effect on the Indians living in the Southwest (*see* Related Books).

4. Read a brief pre-Civil War history of the Southwest (Arizona and New Mexico).

5. Ask the students to read the title and look at the picture on the cover of the book. Ask them these questions:
   What do you think the story is going to be about?
   Who do you think the main characters are going to be?
   What do you think is the setting of the story?

VOCABULARY/DISCUSSION QUESTIONS

Chapters 1-4:

Vocabulary:

mesa (p. 1)	canyon (p. 1)
pinon trees (p. 1)	month of the deer (p. 1)
barrancas (p. 1)	shepherd (p. 3)
aspen grove (p. 4)	corral (p. 6)
mesquite (p. 8)	leagues (p. 8)
lance (p. 8)	goading (p. 11)
Utes (p. 11)	haughty (p. 14)
antelope (p. 14)	Fort Defiance (p. 15)
hogan (p. 15)	Spaniards (p. 17)
plunder (p. 17)	foolhardy (p. 17)
ewes (p. 20)	lamb (verb) (p. 20)
as the eagle flies (p. 22)	slavers (p. 22)
Navaho (p. 22)	Canyon de Chelly (p. 22)
thong (p. 22)	

Questions:

1. Why does Bright Morning leave the sheep? How does her mother respond? Is her mother punishing her or teaching her? Explain your answer. Why does this work?

2. In chapter 2 Bright Morning's friends tease her about Tall Boy. What do they want her to say about him?

3. What do you think Bright Morning's mother really thinks of Tall Boy?

4. Why is raiding the Utes different from raiding the white men?

5. What is the relationship between the Navahos and the Long Knives? Between the Navahos and the Spaniards?

6. Prediction: What will happen to Bright Morning and her friends?

Chapters 5-11:

Vocabulary:

hobble the horses (p. 25)	Jicarilla Apache (p. 29)
blood brothers (p. 29)	Nez Perce (p. 30)
camisa (p. 32)	disposition (p. 32)
pigeon-toed (p. 33)	Kiowas (p. 33)

(vocabulary continues on next page)

Sing Down the Moon / 225

Comanches (p. 33)
Hopis (p. 33)
haggle (p. 35)
adobe (p. 35)
velveteen (p. 38)
fiesta (p. 43)
cunning (p. 44)
tortillas (p. 45)
tethered (p. 47)
pintos (p. 47)
bridle and bit (p. 52)
draw (p. 56)
medicine man (p. 61)

Zunis (p. 33)
Anglos (p. 35)
senora (p. 35)
omen (p. 37)
baile (p. 39)
Jesus Christo (p. 43)
vengeful (p. 44)
Penitentes (p. 46)
turquoise (p. 47)
cactus thorns (p. 48)
burro (p. 52)
ravine (p. 58)

Questions:

1. How does Bright Morning respond to being taken by the slavers?

2. Why do Rosita and Nehana respond so differently to captivity?

3. What kind of a person is the woman who buys Bright Morning?

4. Reread pages 46-49. Why did Nehana choose this particular time and place from which to make their escape?

5. Prediction: What do you think will happen once they return to the village?

Chapters 12-18:

Vocabulary:

sycamore (p. 63)
womanhood ceremony (p. 66)
tunic (p. 67)
comely (p. 69)
portals (p. 91)
Fort Sumner (p. 100)

gaunt (p. 63)
Kin-nadl-dah (p. 67)
buckskin (p. 67)
yucca (p. 69)
Bosque Redondo (p. 100)

Questions:

1. Reread the account of the womanhood ceremony in chapter 13. What are a woman's responsibilities in the Navaho tribe?

2. On page 71, Tall Boy tells Bright Morning, "You think that I went to the white man's village just to rescue you. You are wrong. I went there for another reason." Why do you think he tells her this?

3. Read the last four paragraphs on page 79. Bright Morning sees "a look of shame, or was it anger?" in Tall Boy's eyes. Which do you think it was? Explain.

4. Why didn't the Navahos leave when the Long Knives posted the notice on the tree?

5. Look at a map of Arizona and New Mexico. Locate Canyon de Chelly and Fort Sumner. Discuss the amount of time it took to make this long journey.

6. How do the attitudes of Bright Morning's mother and father differ? Why?

7. Why do you think Bright Morning becomes so attached to Meadow Flower at this particular time?

8. Why do you think Bright Morning's mother cries when she sees Bosque Redondo when she has not cried up until this point in the journey?

Chapters 19-Postscript:

Vocabulary:

driftwood (p. 102)
scalp (p. 105)
lice (p. 105)
treaties (p. 135)
Arizona (p. 135)
massacre (p. 137)
Arapahoes (p. 137)
Chignons (p. 137)

quarrelsome (p. 103)
nits (p. 105)
ramparts (p. 129)
Colonel Kit Carson (p. 135)
pillaged (p. 136)
volunteers (p. 137)
Cheyennes (p. 137)

Questions:

1. Trace Tall Boy's changing attitude throughout this section of the book, beginning with his fatalism at the end of chapter 19 ("The gods will tell us what to do") to his decision to escape on page 123.

2. Why does Bright Morning's family finally relent and give their consent for her marriage to Tall Boy?

3. Why is Bright Morning so concerned about her sheep?

4. Why does Bright Morning break her son's toy spear?

RELATED BOOKS

Alexander, Marthaun. *Weaving on Cardboard: Simple Looms to Make and Use.* New York: Taplinger, 1972.

Armer, Laura Adams. *Waterless Mountain.* New York: David McKay Co., 1931.

Callaway, Sydney M., et al. *Grandfather Stories of the Navajos.* Phoenix: Navajo Curriculum Center Press, 1974.

Carpenter, Allan. *The New Enchantment of America: Arizona.* Chicago: Children's Press, 1978.

_____. *The New Enchantment of America: New Mexico.* Chicago: Children's Press, 1978.

Erdoes, Richard. *The Native Americans: Navajos.* New York: Sterling Publishing Co., 1978.

Georgakas, Dan. *Red Shadows: The History of Native Americans from 1600 to 1900, from the Desert to the Pacific Coast.* Garden City, N.Y.: Doubleday, 1973.

Hausman, Gerald. *Sitting on the Blue-Eyed Bear: Navajo Myths and Legends.* New York: Lawrence Hill & Co., 1975.

Henry, Edna. *Native American Cookbook.* New York: Julian Messner, 1983.

Kelly, Karin. *Weaving.* Minneapolis, Minn.: Lerner, 1973.

Loh, Jules. *Lords of the Earth: A History of the Navajo Indians.* New York: Crowell-Collier Press, 1971.

Maher, Ramona. *Alice Yazzie's Year.* New York: Coward, McCann & Geoghegan, 1977.

Miles, Miska. *Annie and the Old One.* Boston: Little, Brown, 1971.

Nabokov, Peter, ed. *Native American Testimony: An Anthology of Indian and White Relations— First Encounter to Dispossession.* New York: Crowell, 1978.

O'Dell, Scott. *Alexandra.* Boston: Houghton Mifflin 1984.

_____. *The Amethyst Ring.* Boston: Houghton Mifflin, 1983.

_____. *The Black Pearl.* Boston: Houghton Mifflin, 1967.

_____. *Black Star, Bright Dawn.* Boston: Houghton Mifflin, 1988.

_____. *The Captive.* Boston: Houghton Mifflin, 1979.

_____. *Carlotta.* Boston: Houghton Mifflin, 1977.

_____. *Child of Fire.* Boston: Houghton Mifflin, 1974.

_____. *The Feathered Serpent.* Boston: Houghton Mifflin, 1981.

_____. *The Hawk That Dare Not Hunt by Day.* Boston: Houghton Mifflin, 1975.

_____. *Island of the Blue Dolphins.* Boston: Houghton Mifflin, 1961.

_____. *The King's Fifth.* Boston: Houghton Mifflin, 1966.

_____. *The Road to Damietta.* Boston: Houghton Mifflin, 1985.

_____. *Sarah Bishop.* Boston: Houghton Mifflin, 1980.

_____. *The Serpent Never Sleeps.* Boston: Houghton Mifflin, 1987.

_____. *The Spanish Smile.* Boston: Houghton Mifflin, 1982.

_____. *Streams to the River.* Boston: Houghton Mifflin, 1986.

_____. *The Treasure of Topo-el-Bampo.* Boston: Houghton Mifflin, 1976.

_____. *Zia.* Boston: Houghton Mifflin, 1976.

Robinson, Maudie: *Children of the Sun: The Pueblos, Navajos, and Apaches of New Mexico.* New York: Simon & Schuster, 1973.

Roessel, Robert A., and Dillon Platero, eds. *Coyote Stories of the Navajo People.* Phoenix: Navajo Curriculum Center Press, 1974.

Williams, Jeanne. *Trails of Tears: American Indians Driven from Their Lands.* New York: Putnam, 1972. (*See* chapter 4, "The Navajo: The Long Walk.")

ENRICHMENT ACTIVITIES

Sing Down the Moon

1. Compare the life of the Navahos in the book to the life the Navahos lead now. Write a report telling which things have changed and which things have stayed the same.

2. Build a model of a hogan.

3. Compare and contrast the Navaho, Pueblo, and Apache. Include religion, type of shelter, social structure, tribal structure, traditional dress, livelihood, and art. Make a chart to help you share the information with the group.

4. Research Navaho folklore and mythology. Read several tales to see if you can pick out recurring themes. Share the information with the group.

5. Select one of the Navaho folktales. Rewrite it as a play and perform it for the group.

6. Research The Long March. Write a report summarizing its causes and effects.

7. Make two maps of the southwestern United States: one showing where the Indian tribes mentioned in the book were located before the 1860s, and the other one showing where these tribes are located now.

8. Write diary entries that might have been written by a Navaho Indian during The Long March.

9. Research the Anasazi Indians. Draw a series of pictures that will help you report your findings to the group.

10. Make a three-dimensional display or drawing of some of the geological features of the southwestern United States. Include a mesa, canyon, draw, ravine, and plateau.

11. Learn more about Navaho weaving patterns and techniques. Make a simple loom and weave a small rug (*see* Related Books).

12. Cook a meal of Navaho foods (*see* Related Books).

13. Read another book by Scott O'Dell.

14. Create your own activity for *Sing Down the Moon.*

Author/Title Index

Altogether, One at a Time (Konigsburg), 39
Banks, Lynne Reid, 153
Bauer, Marion Dane, 168
The Beast in Ms. Rooney's Room (Giff), 5
Brenner, Barbara, 33
Cameron, Ann, 17
The Celery Stalks at Midnight (Howe), 44
Coerr, Eleanor, 113
Dragonwings (Yep), 173
Eager, Edward, 97
The Egypt Game (Snyder), 123
Enright, Elizabeth, 130
Estes, Eleanor, 50
Fitzhugh, Louise, 207
Follow My Leader (Garfield), 77
Fritz, Jean, 199
Gardiner, John Reynolds, 68
Garfield, James B., 77
Giff, Patricia Reiley, 5
The Gingerbread Rabbit (Jarrell), 10
Gone-Away Lake (Enright), 130
Gormley, Beatrice, 162
Harriet Tubman: Conductor on the Underground Railroad (Petry), 136
The Hero and the Crown (McKinley), 182
Homecoming (Voigt), 192
Homer Price (McCloskey), 83
Homesick: My Own Story (Fritz), 199
Howe, James, 44
The Hundred Dresses (Estes), 50
In the Year of the Boar and Jackie Robinson (Lord), 146
The Indian in the Cupboard (Banks), 153
Jarrell, Randall, 10
Jennifer, Hecate, Macbeth, William McKinley, and Me, Elizabeth (Konigsburg), 91
Julian's Glorious Summer (Cameron), 17
Jumanji (Van Allsburg), 22
Knight's Castle (Eager), 97
Konigsburg, E. L., 39, 91
Levy, Elizabeth, 29
Lord, Bette Bao, 146
MacDonald, Betty, 105
Mail-Order Wings (Gormley), 162
Mathis, Sharon Bell, 65
McCloskey, Robert, 83
McKinley, Robin, 182
Mrs. Piggle-Wiggle's Magic (MacDonald), 105
Nate the Great and the Fishy Prize (Sharmat), 25
Nobody's Family Is Going to Change (Fitzhugh), 207
O'Dell, Scott, 223
On My Honor (Bauer), 168
On the Banks of Plum Creek (Wilder), 55
Petry, Ann, 136
Roll of Thunder, Hear My Cry (Taylor), 216
Sadako and the Thousand Paper Cranes (Coerr), 113
Sharmat, Marjorie Weinman, 25
Sidewalk Story (Mathis), 65
Sing Down the Moon (O'Dell), 223
Smith, Doris Buchanan, 72
Snyder, Zilpha Keatley, 123
Something Queer at the Library (Levy), 29
Song of the Trees (Taylor), 118
Stone Fox (Gardiner), 68
A Taste of Blackberries (Smith), 72
Taylor, Mildred D., 118, 216
Van Allsburg, Chris, 22
Voigt, Cynthia, 192
Wagon Wheels (Brenner), 33
Wilder, Laura Ingalls, 55
Yep, Laurence, 173

028.535 JEN
Jenkins, Christine, 1949-
Novel experiences :
literature units for book
KIN

DISCARD